The Invisible Frame:

How the Overton Window Shapes Society

Winston Vane

"The smart way to keep people passive and obedient is to strictly limit the spectrum of acceptable opinion, but allow very lively debate within that spectrum—even encourage the more critical and dissident views. That gives people the sense that there's free thinking going on, while all the time the presuppositions of the system are being reinforced by the limits put on the range of the debate."

--Noam Chomsky

Winston Vane

Table of Contents

Introduction

What if the most pivotal decisions about our world arise not from government halls but from the invisible parameters of public opinion? This question lies at the heart of "The Invisible Frame," a journey into the unseen realm of the Overton Window.

The Overton Window, named after policy analyst Joseph Overton, represents the range of ideas deemed acceptable in public discourse at any given time. It's a powerful force that shapes our society, often without our conscious awareness. Consider how quickly public opinion on climate change has shifted in recent years, or how social justice movements have redefined our collective understanding of equality.

These changes didn't happen overnight. They're the result of gradual shifts in what we, as a society, consider acceptable or possible. The civil rights movement of the 1960s, for instance, didn't just change laws; it fundamentally altered what Americans believed about racial equality.

Understanding the Overton Window is crucial because it affects every aspect of our lives, from the policies we support to the social norms we adhere to. It's the invisible frame through which we view our world, influencing our decisions, beliefs, and the very fabric of our society.

But here's the exciting part: once you recognize the Overton Window, you can influence it. You have the power to shape public opinion, to move the boundaries of what's considered possible or acceptable. This book will equip you with the knowledge and tools to do just that, empowering you to become an active participant in shaping our collective future.

As we explore the mechanics of the Overton Window, you'll discover how to recognize its influence in your daily life and learn strategies to leverage it for positive change. Are you ready to peek behind the curtain and see the invisible forces shaping our world? Let's begin.

Winston Vane

Chapter 1: The Hidden Framework—Understanding the Overton Window

Origins of the Concept

The Overton Window is a fascinating way to look at how societal norms come and go. It was created by Joseph P. Overton, a political scientist who was curious about how ideas move from being considered extreme to becoming part of everyday discussions. While working with the Mackinac Center for Public Policy in the 1990s, Overton discovered important insights about how society accepts or rejects different concepts. The Overton Window isn't just a dry theory; it's a valuable tool for anyone wanting to understand how public opinion changes over time.

At the heart of Overton's idea is the belief that the acceptance of any idea depends not just on its value but also on how the public views it. This creates an interesting mix of personal beliefs, societal expectations, and the mood of the times. The Overton Window helps outline what topics are okay to talk about in any given time period. Ideas can be placed on a scale ranging from 'unthinkable' on one end, moving through 'radical' and 'acceptable,' all the way to 'popular' and 'policy,' where they become laws or common practices.

To truly grasp the importance of the Overton Window, it helps to look back at history and see how different movements have influenced our shared understanding. Take the civil rights movement of the 1960s, for example. Not too long ago, the idea of racial equality was considered radical and far-fetched. Yet, thanks to relentless advocacy and a growing awareness of injustices, perceptions began to change. Leaders like Martin Luther King Jr. and Malcolm X fought tirelessly for this cause, helping to shift what was once seen as an extreme viewpoint into a widely accepted belief. Today, discussions about race, equality, and justice are central to public policy, thanks to their significant contributions.

We can also see the Overton Window at work in the changing attitudes toward LGBTQ+ rights. For many years, advocating for LGBTQ+ individuals was viewed as radical and unacceptable. In fact, homosexuality faced not just stigma but was even criminalized in many places. However, as society began to change in the late 20th century—thanks to brave individuals and welcoming communities—the window opened wider to include acceptance and advocacy. This shift eventually led to the legalization of same-sex marriage in many countries. The movement from exclusion to acceptance highlights the power of changing public perceptions, which can be influenced by factors like media representation, cultural stories, and the unwavering efforts of activists.

Now, let's consider some current issues like climate change and immigration. The Overton Window helps us understand how conversations around these topics have evolved. For instance, climate change was once a fringe topic, but over the years, the urgent need for environmental reform has gained serious attention. Ideas that were once viewed as extreme, like the Green New Deal, are now part of mainstream political discussions. This change shows how regularly addressing issues through various means—whether it's scientific findings, grassroots movements, or even controversial media coverage—can shift what is seen as acceptable to talk about.

The conversation about immigration has seen a similar evolution. In the past, discussions around immigration reform were often limited, with many ideas leaning toward extremes. Today, however, we see more dialogue about pathways to citizenship and the humane treatment of migrants. This shift doesn't just reflect new policies but also highlights how public opinion can change through advocacy, storytelling, and community involvement.

Understanding the Overton Window is powerful because it reveals just how flexible societal norms can be. It allows us to see where current ideas stand along the spectrum of acceptability. By looking at historical examples and current movements, we can better understand the various factors that shape public conversations and recognize our own potential to drive change.

However, as we navigate these changing boundaries, it's important to be aware of the psychological factors at play. Our biases, social conditioning, and emotional reactions all influence how we perceive what is acceptable. Many people may feel pressured to align with prevailing norms, worried about facing social rejection or backlash for holding viewpoints outside of what's currently deemed acceptable. Being aware of these mental processes can help us understand our own choices and how we respond to societal pressures.

In every debate or movement, the Overton Window serves as a reminder that public opinion is not fixed. It encourages us to think critically about ideas, challenge the status quo, and push the limits of what can be discussed. By tracing the historical background of this concept and considering its impact, we can equip ourselves with the knowledge and tools to engage in meaningful conversations and contribute to positive societal change.

Recognizing where current ideas fit within the Overton Window not only helps us join discussions more effectively but also empowers us to advocate for concepts that might currently be seen as 'radical' or 'unthinkable'. Essentially, understanding this framework invites us to actively shape public discourse, fostering a more inclusive and fair future. By thoughtfully engaging with ideas that lie within the shifting boundaries of the Overton Window, we can help influence the direction of societal acceptance and work toward creating a world that aligns with our values and hopes.

The Window in Everyday Life

The Overton Window isn't just a fancy term used in political science; it's a lively concept that shows up in our daily lives. From chats over coffee to heated exchanges on social media, the limits of what people consider acceptable or even possible are constantly changing. This section looks at how the Overton Window influences different parts of our lives—politics, education, media, and social interactions—using real-life examples to highlight its significant impact.

Let's start with politics. Political agendas are often mirrors of the Overton Window at any given time. Ideas that used to seem outrageous can gain support and move into mainstream conversation with the right mix of advocacy, media attention, and public opinion. Take universal healthcare in the United States, for example. At one point, this idea was pushed to the sidelines of political discussion, viewed as too radical. But over the past few decades, the dialogue around healthcare has changed dramatically. The Affordable Care Act, often referred to as Obamacare, marked a pivotal moment that brought the idea of healthcare as a right into the spotlight. Now, as healthcare costs climb and many people express dissatisfaction with the current system, the idea of Medicare for All is being openly discussed among politicians and policymakers—something that would have seemed impossible not too long ago.

Education is another area where the Overton Window makes a noticeable impact. The conversations we have about changes in curriculum, school reforms, and teaching methods show how societal values shape what is taught and how it's presented. For instance, look at the current debates about teaching critical race theory in schools. What started as a niche academic topic has exploded into national conversations about race, history, and education. Some folks believe critical race theory is essential for understanding systemic racism, while others think it's an extreme ideology that doesn't belong in K-12 education. This back-and-forth highlights how the Overton Window can shift based on public opinion, activism, and political forces, ultimately changing the educational landscape.

The media plays a crucial role as both a reflection and a driver of the Overton Window. With the rise of social media, ideas can spread like wildfire, giving a platform to voices that might otherwise go unheard. Consider the recent focus on mental health. Not long ago, issues surrounding mental health were often met with stigma and misunderstanding, seen as personal flaws or viewed with skepticism. Terms like "nervous breakdown" or "hysteria" were common, creating a culture that shamed those struggling with mental health issues. Thanks to the dedicated efforts of advocates, celebrities, and everyday people sharing their experiences, this narrative has changed dramatically.

Today, mental health is widely recognized as a vital part of overall wellness, and conversations about anxiety, depression, and therapy are becoming more common.

Campaigns like Bell Let's Talk in Canada and social media movements like #MentalHealthAwareness have played a huge role in normalizing these discussions. The Overton Window has widened to include a richer understanding of mental health, enabling conversations that were once considered off-limits to gain visibility. This change not only reflects shifting societal attitudes but also showcases how sharing personal stories can lead to a more inclusive view of health and wellness.

In our everyday interactions, we often support or push against the Overton Window without even realizing it. The small decisions we make—what we talk about with friends, how we react to controversial comments, or the causes we choose to champion—help shape the conversation around societal norms. Reflecting on personal experiences can shine a light on how we interact with the Overton Window. Picture a dinner party where one guest makes a bold statement about immigration policies. The reactions from others can either reinforce that opinion or challenge it. If everyone remains quiet or nods in agreement, they're keeping the window right where it is. But if someone speaks up to question that statement or offer a different view, they're nudging the boundaries of what's considered acceptable dialogue.

Everyday discussions can be snapshots of broader societal changes, showing how individuals can influence the Overton Window in their own circles. Think about a workplace where discussions around diversity and inclusion have generally been limited to HR rules. If a few employees begin sharing their personal experiences related to race, gender, or sexual orientation, a topic that was once uncomfortable might start to feel more acceptable. Over time, this can create an environment where everyone feels encouraged to speak up, eventually leading to changes in company policies and culture.

However, wrestling with the Overton Window isn't always easy. The same forces that allow for the broadening of conversation can also keep outdated or harmful perspectives firmly in place. Consider social media, where echo chambers can develop, reinforcing narrow viewpoints. When algorithms focus on content that matches users' existing beliefs, the Overton Window can shrink, limiting exposure to a wide range of ideas. Recognizing this is vital; it reminds us to actively seek out different viewpoints and challenge our own biases. By doing this, we can help create a healthier public dialogue that promotes understanding and drives change.

Additionally, outside events can also sway the Overton Window. Global crises often shift societal norms and expectations. Take the COVID-19 pandemic, for example; it reshaped conversations about public health, remote work, and social safety nets. Ideas that were previously dismissed, like paid sick leave for all workers or universal basic income, suddenly gained traction as millions faced job losses and economic fears. The urgency of the situation opened the Overton Window, allowing for fresh ideas about social support systems to be considered.

As you think about these examples, take a moment to consider your own role within this framework. Each person has the power to either support or challenge the Overton Window through their actions and choices. Engaging in conversations, sharing personal stories, or standing up for marginalized issues can all help shift the boundaries of acceptable dialogue. Recognizing that each of us has this power is empowering; it encourages people to see themselves as active players in the ongoing evolution of societal norms.

Society thrives on conversation, and the Overton Window reminds us that ideas are always in motion. They change and adapt based on collective action, strategic advocacy, and the daily exchanges we have. By grasping how the Overton Window works in different areas of our lives, we can navigate societal changes more effectively and contribute to meaningful conversations that shape our world.

Moreover, as we witness the ongoing transformation of societal norms, the value of empathy is crystal clear. Engaging with others' views, especially those that differ from our own, nurtures a more inclusive atmosphere. It invites curiosity and understanding, encouraging us to explore ideas that might initially feel out of reach. This openness paves the way for growth, both personally and as a community.

The Overton Window is a powerful tool for understanding how societal norms shift over time. It encourages us to reflect on our experiences and interactions while recognizing the impact our voices can have. Whether through political advocacy, educational reform, media influence, or personal conversations, each of us plays a part in the broader dialogue that shapes our communities. By acknowledging our individual power, we can empower ourselves and others to push for change, helping to build a society that aligns with our values and dreams. Every conversation, every story shared, and every perspective welcomed can play a role in redefining what is acceptable, making space for new ideas that reflect the rich complexity of our shared humanity.

Psychology of Acceptance

In the grand theater of public opinion, the shifts within the Overton Window aren't just about politics or how the media portrays things; they are deeply connected to how we accept ideas. This psychological backdrop serves as both the stage and the script for the unfolding drama of our societal norms and beliefs. By understanding what's happening in our minds, we can see why some ideas take off while others are left behind in the shadows.

At the core of this journey is the idea of cognitive biases—those mental shortcuts that can lead us to make poor decisions. One powerful bias is confirmation bias. This is where people tend to look for information that supports what they already believe while ignoring anything that challenges them. Picture someone who has a strong opinion about climate change. They might gravitate toward news stories, social media posts, and studies that back up their views, while brushing aside evidence that suggests otherwise. This selective attention not only strengthens their beliefs but also expands the Overton Window around ideas they find acceptable, while simultaneously narrowing it around ideas they reject.

Another cognitive bias at play is the bandwagon effect. This describes how we often adopt beliefs or behaviors just because others are doing it. Think of how a new trend on social media can suddenly become the "in" thing. One moment, a specific fashion or idea is only popular among a small group; then, thanks to influencers and peer pressure, it bursts into the mainstream. This bandwagon effect is especially strong in politics. A candidate might gain popularity not just for their policies but also because people see others rallying behind them, creating an illusion that they are widely accepted.

Groupthink is yet another psychological phenomenon that influences what ideas are seen as acceptable in society. This happens when people in a group prioritize harmony and conformity over critical thinking. For example, in a corporate boardroom, if everyone agrees with one viewpoint without discussing alternatives, any dissenting opinions might be silenced. This not only stifles creativity but also reinforces the prevailing norms—ideas that gain acceptance simply because they are repeated by the majority, regardless of their value.

Social conditioning is a powerful force that shapes how we perceive acceptance. From a young age, we learn what is considered acceptable behavior, thoughts, and expressions. These societal norms are reinforced by cultural narratives, traditions, and media representations, acting like gatekeepers to the Overton Window. For instance, when certain groups are portrayed negatively in movies and television, it can perpetuate stereotypes and biases, making it harder for those communities to gain acceptance and recognition.

On a brighter note, media can also spark change by challenging established norms. The rise of diverse voices in film, literature, and journalism has opened up discussions that were once ignored. Documentaries that highlight the realities of climate change or the struggles faced by marginalized communities invite us to rethink our views, pushing the boundaries of the Overton Window. When we encounter stories that differ from our own, it can lead to significant shifts in perspective, fostering greater empathy and understanding.

Social media, in particular, has changed how we see acceptance in incredible ways. Platforms like Twitter, Instagram, and TikTok give even the most niche ideas a chance to shine, potentially bringing them into the spotlight. Movements like #MeToo and #BlackLivesMatter have ignited worldwide conversations about issues that used to be pushed aside. However, there's a downside; social media can also create echo chambers where people only hear opinions that mirror their own. This can narrow the Overton Window, making it tough for differing views to be heard above the chatter.

As we navigate this intricate web of psychology and societal norms, it becomes clear that developing strategies to overcome our cognitive biases is important. One of our best tools is critical thinking. By questioning our beliefs and the information we absorb, we can start to break down the barriers created by confirmation bias. This means seeking out different perspectives, even those that make us uncomfortable. It's about engaging in self-reflection and truly examining the reasons behind our beliefs.

Creating an environment where open conversation is encouraged can help alleviate the effects of groupthink. By allowing dissenting voices to be heard—whether in workplaces, classrooms, or online spaces—we can foster more comprehensive discussions and innovative ideas. These conversations can help expand the Overton Window by making once-taboo topics more acceptable and open for discussion.

Engaging in active questioning means not only looking closely at our own beliefs but also considering the larger societal narratives that shape our thoughts. By becoming more aware of the cultural norms and media influences that mold our acceptance of certain ideas, we can start to challenge those narratives. This awareness empowers us to actively shape societal norms rather than passively consume them.

Moreover, we can't overlook the importance of empathy in this process. When we take the time to listen to others' experiences and viewpoints, we gain a richer understanding of the complexities behind societal issues. Empathy can bridge divides and widen the boundaries of the Overton Window. By engaging with ideas that initially seem strange or unacceptable, we open ourselves up to the possibility of change.

The psychology of acceptance teaches us that societal norms are not fixed; they are constantly evolving. Each of us has the power to influence these norms through our actions, choices, and interactions. By recognizing our individual power, we can encourage a more inclusive dialogue that invites diverse viewpoints and challenges the status quo. It is this readiness to engage, reflect, and question that will ultimately help us move toward progress and positive change.

By fostering critical thinking and empathy, we equip ourselves to navigate the complexities of the Overton Window with confidence and purpose. We can become informed participants in the larger conversations that shape our communities and the world. The journey toward acceptance may have its hurdles, but each step we take toward understanding and questioning leads to a broader dialogue that can reshape societal norms for the better.

As we reflect on the implications of the psychology of acceptance, let's think about our individual roles in this dynamic landscape. Are we passive observers, accepting whatever ideas come our way? Or are we active participants, challenging and reshaping the norms that influence our thoughts and actions? The answers to these questions will help guide us as we navigate the intricacies of societal acceptance and work toward a fairer and more just future.

Chapter 2: History's Shifting Windows

The Overton Window: A Historical Framework

Understanding the Overton Window is like peering through a lens that helps us see the quiet yet powerful forces that influence what society considers acceptable over time. This framework is a valuable tool for grasping how ideas move from the edges of public conversation to the heart of social acceptance. The Overton Window isn't fixed; it shifts and grows, reflecting society's changing attitudes, beliefs, and values. By paying attention to its movements, we can better recognize how significant social movements have not only swayed public opinion but also sparked profound changes in the very fabric of our society.

At its heart, the Overton Window outlines what kinds of thoughts are accepted in society at any given time. Ideas that lie outside this window are often seen as extreme or out of place, while those within it are considered normal and widely embraced. This concept has deep historical roots, tracing back through various social, political, and cultural movements that have dramatically reshaped public opinion. Throughout history, certain moments have acted as turning points, pushing the Overton Window to expand or shrink, thus altering what is seen as acceptable and appropriate by society.

Take the Women's Suffrage Movement, for example. This significant campaign fought tirelessly for women's right to vote. At the beginning of the 20th century, the idea that women should have the same voting rights as men was often dismissed as absurd. It challenged long-standing gender roles and societal expectations. However, as determined activists advocated for their cause, they gradually changed how people viewed these ideas. What was once considered radical evolved into a fundamental human right. This journey highlights the strength of advocacy and activism in pushing the Overton Window, allowing once-dismissed ideas to gain ground and eventually become accepted.

The Civil Rights Era offers another clear illustration of the Overton Window at work. During the mid-20th century, racial segregation and discrimination were deeply ingrained in American society. The fight against racial injustice became a monumental struggle, challenging a system that had long tolerated inequality. Activists, fueled by a vision for a fairer society, rallied to address the racism that affected every aspect of life. As they garnered support and attention, public awareness began to shift, revealing the harsh realities faced by African Americans and other marginalized groups. Events like the Montgomery Bus Boycott, the March on Washington, and the passage of crucial laws such as the Civil Rights Act of 1964 played key roles in moving the Overton Window toward acceptance of equality and justice for all, regardless of race.

The LGBTQ+ Rights movement also shows how flexible the Overton Window can be. For many years, individuals in the LGBTQ+ community faced discrimination, exclusion, and violence, with their identities pushed out of the public eye. The fight for same-sex marriage and broader LGBTQ+ rights demonstrated how public opinion could change through storytelling, representation, and the unyielding quest for respect and dignity. As more LGBTQ+ stories came to light, societal attitudes began to shift. What was once considered taboo gradually gained acceptance, culminating in the landmark Supreme Court ruling in Obergefell v. Hodges in 2015, which affirmed the right to marry for same-sex couples throughout the United States. This moment reflected years of activism and advocacy that expanded the Overton Window, making acceptance and equality essential in today's society.

The connection between historical movements and the Overton Window teaches us that societal norms don't grow in isolation. They are shaped by the combined actions, voices, and experiences of those who challenge the status quo. The struggles from the past remind us that change is possible, showing that the Overton Window can be pushed, widened, and even redefined. Each movement not only affects its own time but also lays the groundwork for future generations to build upon, fostering a more inclusive and just society.

As we look back at history, it's clear that understanding the Overton Window is crucial for anyone wanting to engage meaningfully in social discussions. Recognizing shifts in public opinion and the movements that have sparked those changes empowers us to take part in the ongoing evolution of societal norms. It encourages us to explore how collective voices can amplify and change the conversation, ultimately advocating for a fairer and more just world.

Looking forward, we must reflect on the lessons these movements teach us. The battles for gender equality, racial justice, and LGBTQ+ rights highlight the need for ongoing vigilance and activism as society faces new challenges. As fresh issues arise and old biases resurface, it's our job to recognize the shifting windows of our own time. By understanding the historical context of the Overton Window, we can better navigate the complexities of today's conversations, ensuring our collective efforts guide us toward a more inclusive and caring society.

As we journey through history, it's important to appreciate how interconnected these movements are. Each fight informs the next, creating a rich dialogue that spans generations. The Overton Window reminds us that progress is not just a possibility; it often results from relentless determination and the bravery to question the dominant narratives. By looking at the historical framework of the Overton Window, we uncover the stories of those who stood against oppression, who dared to envision a better world, and who, against all odds, managed to shift the perspectives through which we view society.

This exploration is not just an academic exercise; it's an invitation to connect with the past in a way that informs our present and shapes our future. By recognizing how the Overton Window has been influenced by historical events and movements, we empower ourselves to actively participate in the ongoing evolution of societal norms. As we navigate the complexities of today's world, let's draw inspiration from those who came before us, understanding that we, too, have the power to challenge the limits of the Overton Window and advocate for a more just and equitable society. The road to progress is far from over, and each of us has a crucial role in shaping the narratives that define our world.

Women's Suffrage Movement: Paving the Way for Change

In the exciting journey of civil rights, the Women's Suffrage Movement shines brightly as a symbol of determination, strength, and deep societal change. This movement tells the story of countless women who boldly stood up against the norm, insisting on their right to participate equally in democracy. Spanning from the late 19th century to the hard-won passage of the 19th Amendment in 1920, this story is filled with key figures, important events, and moments of both victory and heartbreak. As we dive into this crucial movement, we will meet inspiring advocates like Susan B. Anthony, Elizabeth Cady Stanton, and Sojourner Truth, and witness how their tireless dedication transformed public views on gender roles and women's rights.

The roots of the Women's Suffrage Movement date back to a time when women were expected to stay at home, with their voices and dreams pushed aside by strict societal expectations. The late 19th century was a time of significant change in the United States, as various movements began to come together, each fighting for the rights of those who were marginalized. Against the backdrop of abolition, temperance, and labor rights, the suffrage movement began to rise, sparked by a growing awareness of the injustices faced by women. A powerful realization took hold: if women wanted to have a chance at equality, they first needed the right to vote.

The Seneca Falls Convention of 1848 is often seen as the spark that ignited the suffrage movement. This gathering brought together activists like Stanton and Anthony, who voiced the grievances of women and laid out their demands for equality. The Declaration of Sentiments, a powerful document created during the convention, boldly stated that "all men and women are created equal," setting the stage for a struggle that would span generations. This convention represented a pivotal moment, marking the first organized effort to advocate for women's rights, but it also signified the beginning of a long and challenging journey filled with obstacles and setbacks.

As the suffrage movement gained steam, its early leaders found themselves navigating a rocky path filled with resistance and societal pushback. They faced not only scorn from those who believed women were unsuited for public life but also divisions within their own ranks. The intersection of race and gender became a particularly sensitive issue, with figures like Sojourner Truth stepping forward to highlight the unique struggles of Black women. In her powerful "Ain't I a Woman?" speech delivered in 1851, Truth challenged the narrow definitions of femininity that overlooked women of color, emphasizing the need for a more inclusive approach to suffrage. Her words struck a chord, reminding suffragists that the fight for women's rights was inseparable from the broader battle for racial equality.

To sway public opinion and change how society viewed women's roles, the suffrage movement developed its own strategies. Grassroots organizing, distributing pamphlets, public speeches, and even parades became vital tools for the suffragists. Anthony and Stanton were particularly skilled at using the media to draw attention to their cause. They crafted compelling stories that framed women's suffrage not just as a political issue, but as a moral necessity. By connecting their fight to the values of justice and equality, they began to move the conversation about women's rights from the sidelines to the forefront.

But as the movement grew stronger, so did the backlash against it. Suffragists faced fierce opposition from various groups determined to uphold traditional gender roles. Concerned by the idea of women stepping outside the home, opponents rallied to put a stop to the suffragists' efforts. Both men and women argued that giving women the right to vote would threaten society and lead to moral decline. These fears were amplified by sensationalist media portrayals that painted suffragists as radicals willing to disrupt the natural order.

Despite these obstacles, the movement kept gaining strength, especially as the nation faced the realities of World War I. The war changed societal expectations, as women filled roles once held only by men, proving their capabilities and grit. The contributions of women during this time—whether in factories, hospitals, or volunteering—began to reshape how people viewed women's roles in society. The argument for suffrage became more urgent as the nation recognized that women deserved the right to vote and were essential to the nation-building efforts.

The years leading up to the passage of the 19th Amendment were filled with intense activism, as suffragists employed various tactics to advance their goals. The National Woman's Party, led by Alice Paul, stood out for its bold approach, organizing protests and picketing the White House. Their efforts peaked with a dramatic demonstration on President Woodrow Wilson's inauguration day in 1913, where thousands marched in support of women's suffrage. This event marked a significant turning point, drawing national attention to the cause and further shifting public perception. As pressure mounted, even President Wilson, once an opponent of women's suffrage, began to see the necessity of supporting the amendment in recognition of women's contributions during the war.

All these efforts culminated on August 26, 1920, when the 19th Amendment was ratified, granting women the right to vote. This victory was hard-won, achieved through decades of relentless advocacy, sacrifice, and unwavering commitment. For many women, this moment was bittersweet; while they had finally secured the right to vote, the battle for true equality was far from over. The suffrage movement had opened the door, but it was just the start of a much larger fight for civil rights.

The legacy of the Women's Suffrage Movement goes well beyond the passage of the 19th Amendment. It laid the groundwork for future civil rights activism, showing that social change is possible through collective action and determination. The women of this movement not only redefined societal norms regarding gender but also paved the way for future generations to build on their achievements. Their victories and struggles serve as important lessons for today's advocates, reminding us that the journey toward equality is ongoing.

Reflecting on the broader impacts of the suffrage movement, it becomes obvious that changes in public perception and societal norms are often met with challenges and resistance. The shifting landscape of beliefs is not a straightforward path; it's shaped by the hard work of those willing to challenge the status quo. The Women's Suffrage Movement beautifully showcased this, as advocates slowly changed the narrative around women's rights, despite facing significant opposition.

This movement also underscores the importance of including diverse voices in social justice efforts. Leaders like Sojourner Truth emphasized that the fight for gender equality cannot happen in isolation. It's crucial to consider the unique experiences and challenges faced by women of color and other marginalized groups. The suffragists' struggle serves as a reminder that true progress requires an inclusive approach that recognizes the interconnectedness of various social justice issues.

By exploring the Women's Suffrage Movement, we uncover a rich history of resilience and advocacy that continues to inspire present-day efforts for gender equality and social justice. The bravery shown by these early activists resonates with us today, urging us to carry their spirit forward in our quest for a fairer society. Their legacy reminds us that the fight for rights and recognition isn't just about one group; it's about advancing the shared humanity that connects us all.

As we look ahead, it's important to remember that the lessons from the suffrage movement remain relevant in our ongoing struggles for social justice. The relentless pursuit of equality requires our commitment, courage, and vigilance. The landscape of beliefs will keep shifting, and we must ensure that the narratives we promote and the movements we support reflect the values of inclusivity and justice for everyone. By honoring the legacy of the women who forged the path for change, we reaffirm our belief in the power of collective action and the undeniable right of every individual to play a role in shaping the society they live in.

The Women's Suffrage Movement not only changed the face of American politics but also built a strong foundation for the ongoing fight for equality. Engaging with the stories of the past reminds us of the resilience of those who dared to dream of a better world and the importance of carrying that spirit into our advocacy today. In every struggle for justice that unfolds, we hear echoes of their fight, witness the shifting of beliefs, and hold onto the hope that change is indeed possible.

Lessons from History: Shifting Paradigms and Future Implications

The story of societal change is made up of many individual threads, each one representing movements, struggles, and victories that together create a powerful narrative of human rights advocacy. When we look back at key moments like the Women's Suffrage Movement, the Civil Rights Era, and the LGBTQ+ Rights Movement, we see how these unique but connected movements have shaped today's social justice landscape. These movements weren't just responses to the injustices of their time; they showed the strength of coming together and the lasting influence of storytelling. They offer us important lessons that still echo in our current challenges, encouraging us to take action on pressing issues such as climate change, immigration, and economic justice.

The connections between these historical movements highlight how public perception evolves. When we think about the Women's Suffrage Movement, it's clear that its successes and hardships were part of a larger journey towards civil rights. The fight for women's right to vote was closely tied to the struggles for abolition, labor rights, and racial equality. This interconnectedness was crucial; it showed that no quest for justice stands alone. Each movement built on the others, pushing the boundaries of what ideas are accepted in the public conversation.

The Civil Rights Movement, which followed the fight for suffrage, further developed the groundwork laid by earlier activists. The determination of leaders like Martin Luther King Jr., Rosa Parks, and Malcolm X resonated with the fight for women's rights, highlighting a common desire for equality. Their efforts changed the narrative about race in America and reshaped what was possible for marginalized communities. Their marches for justice weren't just protests; they were powerful stories that framed their fight as a moral call to the nation's conscience.

The LGBTQ+ Rights Movement grew from the lessons learned in these earlier fights for equality. The Stonewall Riots of 1969 marked a pivotal moment that spurred the modern struggle for LGBTQ+ rights, showing how coming together can change societal norms. Just like the suffragists and civil rights advocates before them, LGBTQ+ activists used storytelling and visibility to confront deep-seated prejudices. By sharing their experiences, they widened the conversation even more, pushing for acceptance and equality in a world that had long pushed them to the sidelines.

As we think about these historical movements, it becomes clear that changing public perception is a slow and often bumpy road. Resistance pops up when old beliefs clash with new ideas. But history has taught us that persistent efforts can lead to incredible changes. The advancements made in women's rights, civil rights for people of color, and LGBTQ+ equality all show how steadfast commitment can overcome obstacles. Each movement reminds us that the path to change isn't straightforward; it's filled with challenges that require resilience and determination.

Today, we stand at a similar crossroads. Issues like climate change and economic justice need our focus and action. The lessons from history tell us that these current struggles need the same energy and unity that characterized the earlier movements. Each person's voice adds to the collective struggle for justice, and it's important to realize that change can start small. Local actions can create ripples that influence the larger societal narrative.

Empathy, education, and advocacy are key to effective societal change.

Understanding and relating to the experiences of others is crucial in a world often split by differing ideologies and identities. We all play a part in shaping the future we desire. Whether we engage in community organizing, join protests, or simply educate ourselves and others, our efforts feed into the broader movement for social justice. By lifting up diverse voices, we can foster a more inclusive dialogue that recognizes the complexity of the issues we face.

As we look to the future, we need to stay alert and proactive. The historical movements that forged paths for change remind us that the fight for justice is ongoing and calls for our constant participation. The Overton Window—the range of ideas considered acceptable—doesn't stand still; it changes as society faces new challenges and beliefs. By understanding how this evolution works, we can better prepare ourselves to impact public discussions in meaningful ways.

It's clear that the collective struggles of the past have created a solid foundation for our understanding of justice today. The stories of those who came before us serve as powerful reminders of our potential to create change, inspiring us to channel that energy into our advocacy. We must remember that the victories gained by earlier movements weren't the end; they were important steps in an unfinished journey. The need for solidarity across different movements is just as critical today, reinforcing the idea that our fights are interconnected.

In this spirit, we can draw strength from the resilience of those who have fought for their rights throughout history. Their unwavering determination can guide us as we face today's challenges. By understanding our place in the ongoing pursuit of justice, we can help build a society that is not only more inclusive but also more compassionate.

We must also recognize the power of storytelling. Each of us can share our experiences, speak out against injustices, and advocate for a fairer world. History shows us that by voicing our stories and engaging in open conversations, we can change perceptions and expand the Overton Window for those who come after us.

Reflecting on the lessons from past struggles reminds us of the duty that comes with this knowledge. Our involvement in today's issues isn't just a personal choice; it's a collective responsibility. The challenges we face today urge us to embrace the lessons of history, acknowledge our role, and work together for a future that upholds the rights and dignity of all individuals.

The chance for transformative social change is within reach. We must cultivate the empathy that fuels our advocacy, educate ourselves and others about the intricacies of social justice, and stay committed to fostering inclusivity. This is a call to action that asks us to step outside our comfort zones and engage with the world around us.

As we move ahead, let's draw strength from the movements that paved the way for us. The stories of suffragists, civil rights advocates, and LGBTQ+ defenders are woven into our shared history, reminding us that progress is achievable through determination and unity. We must carry their legacy forward into the present, using the lessons of the past to guide our actions today.

In doing so, we can help create a future where justice is not just a dream but a reality for everyone. By recognizing our interconnectedness and embracing our roles as advocates for change, we have a tremendous opportunity to challenge the status quo and redefine what's possible. Together, through empathy, education, and united action, we can navigate the complexities of our time and work toward a more just and equitable society for all.

Chapter 3: The Mechanics of Movement

Incrementalism vs. Radical Change

The path to social change is often shaped by the push and pull between two different methods: incrementalism and radical change. Each approach offers a distinct way to create change, and both come with their own strengths and weaknesses. By exploring these ideas, we can better understand what drives shifts in public opinion, how societal norms evolve, and how these changes influence the Overton Window, the range of ideas considered acceptable in public discussion.

Incrementalism moves at a steady, gradual pace, almost like a gentle stream that slowly carves out a canyon over time. This method gives society the chance to adjust and adapt to new ideas, which helps reduce the chances of backlash. History is full of examples, from the long fight for civil rights for marginalized groups to the growing recognition of climate change as a serious issue. Incrementalism often comforts people, presenting changes as reasonable and manageable, which encourages acceptance rather than resistance.

In contrast, radical change is like an earthquake that shakes up society, creating chaos but also paving the way for quick transformation. This approach pushes for immediate, sweeping changes that often challenge established norms and values. Events like the Stonewall Riots, which sparked the LGBTQ+ rights movement, are prime examples of radical change. These riots were not just random acts of rebellion; they expressed a deep desire for freedom from oppression. Unlike the gradual pace of incremental change, radical actions disrupt the status quo, demanding immediate acknowledgment of injustice and rethinking societal structures.

The relationship between these two strategies is intricate, and their effectiveness often depends on the circumstances in which they are used. During the civil rights movement in the United States, leaders like Martin Luther King Jr. promoted nonviolent protest and gradual integration. His approach is a clear example of incrementalism, garnering support while helping society accept the rights of African Americans. On the flip side, the Black Panther Party took a more radical stance, calling for immediate changes, self-defense against oppressive forces, and systemic reform. These different methods show how various strategies can resonate differently with different groups, shaping public perception and shifting the Overton Window.

From a psychological perspective, incrementalism tends to feel more reassuring to people. The idea of gradual change lets individuals digest new concepts without feeling overwhelmed or threatened. It gives them confidence that their world won't change overnight, creating a smoother path to acceptance. On the other hand, radical change can trigger fear and resistance. People might see radical movements as threats to their way of life, leading to backlash that can undermine the goals of those movements. Recognizing this psychological dynamic is important for supporters of either approach, as it can influence how they convey their messages and reach out to their audiences.

Both strategies have their own unique benefits, but they can also be double-edged swords. Incrementalism may build more significant long-term acceptance, but its slow pace can frustrate those eager for immediate changes to social injustices. This frustration can create a sense of urgency that fuels radical movements, forming a cycle where the two strategies influence one another. For instance, the slow progress in the fight for LGBTQ+ rights created the groundwork for the more radical actions seen during Stonewall, while the riots forced incremental changes in policy and public perception.

The impact of these strategies on the Overton Window is profound. This concept refers to the range of ideas that society considers acceptable at any given time. Incrementalism can help expand this window by slowly shifting societal norms to include ideas that were once considered taboo. As people become more familiar with new concepts, these ideas can transition from the fringes to the mainstream. Conversely, radical changes can also shift the Overton Window, but often in a more sudden way. They can bring once-unthinkable ideas into the public conversation, prompting discussions and critiques that challenge society to confront uncomfortable truths.

The relationship between incrementalism and radical change isn't just a theoretical discussion; it plays a crucial role in how social movements succeed or fail. Understanding how to balance these strategies can help individuals and organizations navigate the complex landscape of social change. Activists can advocate for immediate action while also planting the seeds for long-term acceptance. This combined approach can create a ripple effect, enabling movements to connect with a broader audience while staying true to their core beliefs.

Language plays a significant role in shaping conversations about social change. The words we choose can frame debates, influence ideas, and sway public opinion. Terms like "incremental" and "radical" carry different emotional weights, which can affect how movements are perceived. For example, labeling a movement as "radical" might lead to quick dismissal or backlash, while describing it as "progressive" or "evolutionary" can invite acceptance and curiosity. The way we use language is a powerful tool that shapes narratives, impacting the movement of the Overton Window and how new ideas are accepted.

We can see this linguistic influence in the way climate change advocates frame their messages. Phrases like "climate emergency" or "climate crisis" create a sense of urgency and demand immediate action, reflecting a more radical approach. In contrast, terms like "sustainable development" or "environmental stewardship" emphasize a gradual, incremental process of improvement. The choice of words can shape how receptive the public is to a message and what kinds of reactions it generates.

Additionally, the media plays a crucial role in this discussion. Historically, the media has served as a gatekeeper, shaping narratives and determining which ideas gain visibility.

How an issue is framed can greatly impact public perception, either broadening or narrowing the Overton Window. When media outlets spotlight radical movements, they can elevate those ideas to a national stage, forcing society to confront and discuss them. Conversely, when the media ignores certain topics, it can reinforce existing power structures, stifling progressive movements and maintaining the status quo.

Ultimately, understanding how these elements work—the balance between incrementalism and radical change, the psychological aspects involved, the power of language, and the media's role—allows individuals and movements to navigate the challenges of societal change more effectively. By recognizing the interplay between these two approaches, advocates can empower themselves and their communities to participate actively in shaping public discourse. The talk around social change isn't just about the ideas themselves; it's about how we present and frame those ideas to the world.

In summary, the journey toward social change is complex and layered. Incrementalism offers a gentle route to acceptance, allowing the public to adapt gradually to new ideas. Radical change, while disruptive, can trigger significant shifts in public consciousness and motivate necessary action. The relationship between these strategies can either broaden or narrow the Overton Window, revealing the ever-changing nature of societal norms and behaviors. By using language effectively and engaging with media narratives, advocates can work within this framework to inspire change that is both immediate and lasting. Building a more inclusive and just society requires understanding these dynamics, enabling individuals to actively and meaningfully engage in conversations about social change.

Media's Role in Shaping Perception

The way media influences how we see the world is both deep and complex. It acts like a mirror, reflecting the values of our society, while also serving as a sculptor that shapes those values in ways we might not even notice. In an era where information is constantly flowing and opinions are formed in the blink of an eye, the media's ability to create stories is more important than ever. It acts as a gatekeeper, deciding which stories get attention and which ones fade into the background. The narratives formed by the media do more than influence our thoughts; they help mold what topics are considered acceptable to discuss—this concept is often referred to as the Overton Window.

To truly understand how powerful media can be, it's useful to look back at key moments in history when the way news was covered changed public opinion. A great example is the coverage of the Vietnam War. At first, media reports supported the government's view of the conflict, helping people feel positive about military involvement. However, as more raw images and honest accounts of the war reached viewers through television, the story started to change dramatically. The war was no longer seen as a noble cause; it became a painful struggle marked by suffering and moral confusion. The fallout was significant—public opinion shifted, protests erupted across the country, and trust in the government took a huge hit. This change didn't just happen on its own; it was a direct result of how the media chose to tell the story.

The coverage of climate change shows just how much media can shape the conversation around urgent global issues. For a long time, discussions about climate change were often pushed aside or presented as a burden on the economy instead of the pressing moral issue it truly is. But as the media began to focus on devastating weather events and amplify the voices of scientists and activists, the narrative changed. Climate change was no longer seen as a distant problem; it became an immediate crisis that demanded urgent action. This shift in perspective has greatly expanded the Overton Window, moving climate policy discussions from the sidelines of political debates to a central issue that affects elections, policies, and how we behave as a society.

Understanding how media frames its messages reveals the different ways language, visuals, and storytelling can shape what people think. The words chosen to describe events can greatly influence public feelings. For example, calling a group of people protesting against unfair treatment a "riot" brings to mind chaos and violence, often leading to criticism. On the other hand, referring to the same event as a "demonstration" suggests civic duty and legitimacy. These choices in language can shift how audiences perceive the actions, affecting whether they view the protesters as threats or champions of justice.

Visual images also play a crucial role in shaping opinions. Following the Black Lives Matter movement, images of protests, especially those showing police brutality or peaceful demonstrators, dominated the news. These powerful visuals created emotional connections, fostering solidarity and sparking discussions about racial injustice that may not have gained the same traction without those striking images. The impact of visuals can cut through language barriers, conveying feelings in ways that mere words often cannot.

With the rise of social media, the landscape of media influence has changed dramatically. Platforms like Twitter, Facebook, and Instagram have given everyday people the power to share information, allowing grassroots movements to amplify their messages in ways that weren't possible before. This shift in how information is shared has given a voice to those who are often ignored, challenging mainstream narratives. As a result, a wider range of ideas is now part of public discussions, effectively widening the Overton Window.

However, this new power also brings challenges. While social media offers a platform for unheard voices, it can also lead to the rapid spread of misinformation. In a setting where anyone can claim to be an expert, distinguishing between credible information and falsehoods can become tricky. This confusing environment complicates public conversations, making it harder for individuals to navigate the many conflicting stories vying for their attention.

The stakes are high. The ease of spreading misinformation undermines trust in traditional media, leading people to turn to more familiar, often biased sources for news. This fragmentation creates echo chambers, where individuals only encounter ideas that reinforce what they already believe, further narrowing the Overton Window. The challenge then becomes promoting critical media literacy—an understanding of how to analyze and question the narratives we encounter in our daily lives.

To navigate this complicated media landscape, individuals need to develop a critical eye, questioning the motivations behind the stories they consume. Recognizing media's role in shaping narratives empowers people to engage more thoughtfully in social discussions. By examining the language used, the visuals presented, and the underlying motives behind a story, one can better understand the intentions behind the information they receive.

For instance, climate change activists have increasingly acknowledged the power of language in their messaging. By shifting from terms like "global warming" to "climate crisis," they aim to present the issue as urgent, encouraging audiences to take action rather than remain passive. This change in language reflects a deeper understanding of how framing can inspire action, influence policy, and shift public awareness.

It's also important to recognize the role traditional media plays in this equation. While social media has transformed how information is shared, traditional outlets like newspapers, television news, and radio still have a significant impact on public opinion. The challenges they face in this fast-changing media landscape are significant. As they work to maintain their credibility, the choices they make in framing issues can create waves that go far beyond their immediate audience.

In the end, the relationship between media, public perception, and the Overton Window is dynamic and always changing. The stories crafted by media not only shape individual beliefs but also influence societal norms and expectations. Grasping the nuances of this relationship is crucial for anyone who wants to engage meaningfully in discussions about social change. By promoting media literacy and critical engagement, individuals can empower themselves and their communities to navigate the complexities of today's discourse, ensuring that a variety of voices are heard and that the narratives shaping our reality reflect the values we hold dear.

In this era of information overload, it's more vital than ever for people to be mindful consumers of media. By questioning stories, analyzing language, and understanding the motivations behind the information we receive, we can reclaim the ability to shape the conversations around the issues that matter most. As we participate in societal debates, let's keep in mind that the narratives we share and amplify have the power to impact the world—not just for ourselves, but for future generations as well.

Language and Framing

Language is not just a collection of words thrown together; it's the very building block of how we tell our stories, understand our experiences, and take action. The words we choose have a huge impact on how we communicate and how we view the world. This is especially true when it comes to social issues, where the way we frame our language can greatly shape what people think, how they feel, and, ultimately, how society moves forward.

To really grasp how powerful language can be in shaping conversations, we need to recognize that framing isn't simply a neutral act—it's deeply political. When an issue is introduced to the public, the words and narratives surrounding that issue can sway opinions and influence behavior. This idea is captured in the Overton Window, a concept that describes the range of ideas considered acceptable in public debate. As the way we talk about issues changes, so too does the Overton Window. This allows some topics to become part of mainstream discussions while others get pushed aside.

Take the term "climate change" as an example. At first, this phrase was mainly used in scientific circles, often overshadowed by more immediate concerns like economic growth or energy needs. The public conversation around it was limited, with only a small audience of environmentalists and scholars engaging deeply in the topic. Over time, however, activists and communicators began to see the need to change the narrative. By shifting from a clinical, scientific term to more urgent phrases like "climate crisis" or "climate emergency," they created a sense of urgency that stirred public opinion. Suddenly, climate change wasn't just a distant concept— it became a pressing issue that called for collective action. This reframing expanded the Overton Window, pushing climate issues to the forefront of political and social discussions around the globe.

But language can also be used in harmful ways, reinforcing negative views and slowing down progress. In discussions about social justice, for instance, the term "political correctness" is often brandished like a weapon against those advocating for more inclusive language and practices. Critics frequently use it to dismiss calls for thoughtfulness, framing them as overreactions or burdensome demands, which in turn hampers movements aimed at making spaces safer for marginalized communities. This illustrates a vital point: language not only shapes discussions but also mirrors larger cultural shifts. As society progresses, so too does our understanding of what respectful and appropriate language looks like. The debates around political correctness highlight the tension between progress and tradition, and between innovation and conservatism.

Looking at how language impacts advocacy gives us more examples of its power. For instance, the pro-choice movement has worked hard to change the conversation surrounding abortion. By focusing the narrative on bodily autonomy and reproductive rights rather than just the act of terminating a pregnancy, advocates aim to foster empathy and understanding. This shift makes it harder to view the issue solely as "abortion" and instead connects it to broader themes of personal freedom and women's rights. The language used by both sides significantly shapes public beliefs about morality, legality, and individual agency.

We can also analyze the effects of language through successful and unsuccessful campaigns. Consider the "War on Drugs." This phrase itself creates a sense of urgency and righteousness, framing substance abuse as part of a larger battle. The language used here affects how the public views drug users and drives policy decisions that often favor punishment over compassion. The fallout has been severe, leading to mass incarceration and stigma around addiction. This framing constricts the Overton Window, allowing only a narrow view of drug use as a criminal issue rather than a public health matter.

On the other hand, campaigns like "Defund the Police" show how framing can be a double-edged sword. At first glance, the phrase might sound extreme or even chaotic, conjuring images of lawlessness for critics. Yet, supporters use this bold language to challenge the status quo and spark a broader dialogue about reallocating funds toward community services, mental health support, and education. While the initial shock value might cause resistance, the deeper goal is to change how society thinks about public safety and justice. The challenge is conveying the complexities and intentions behind such language effectively.

The way language works in activism relies heavily on how it's received by different audiences. Activists need to carefully balance bold calls for action with the risk of pushing away potential supporters through divisive language. This makes understanding the audience crucial. A passionate statement can light a fire under a committed group, but it might also scare off those who are undecided. Finding that balance between fervent advocacy and clear communication is an important skill for effective activism.

With social media on the rise, the stakes have become even higher. These platforms provide a unique chance for activists to reach the public directly, bypassing traditional media gatekeepers. But they also create a noisy environment filled with competing stories. In this setting, language becomes even more critical. Memes, hashtags, and short phrases can simplify complex messages into bite-sized pieces, sometimes at the expense of important details. The challenge is to maintain clarity and substance while also making an emotional connection with a wide array of people.

A shining example of this is the #MeToo movement, which has become a powerful force in the fight against sexual harassment and assault. The language surrounding this movement—terms like "survivor," "consent," and "toxic masculinity"—has altered societal conversations about gender dynamics and violence. By framing personal stories of trauma as part of a collective fight for justice, the movement has broadened the understanding of systemic issues and built solidarity among people from different backgrounds. This shift in language has expanded the Overton Window, allowing discussions that were once considered taboo to become part of everyday conversations.

However, the backlash against the movement underscores how precarious these language shifts can be. The phrase "believe survivors" became a rallying cry, but it also faced criticism for allegedly undermining the presumption of innocence. This tension reveals how language can become a battleground, with competing sides struggling for control over words and meanings. Advocates for change must stay alert, as public opinion can be vulnerable to misinterpretation or misrepresentation.

Understanding the broader impact of language goes beyond activism. In politics, the use of euphemisms, jargon, and coded phrases can subtly alter perceptions of policies and issues. Take the phrase "collateral damage," for example. This term sanitizes the pain caused by military actions, allowing people to engage with complex ethical issues without facing the harsh truths of war. Such language can desensitize audiences to the consequences of violence, making it easier to back aggressive policies that might otherwise provoke moral outrage.

Similarly, the language used around immigration has seen significant shifts. Politicians and media frequently use terms like "illegal alien" or "undocumented migrant" to paint the issue of immigration in stark, black-and-white terms. These terms carry powerful connotations—one suggests criminality, while the other evokes empathy. By examining the language in these discussions, we can uncover underlying biases that shape how the public feels about immigration policy and reform.

The implications of language also reach into the business world, where how things are framed can affect consumer behavior and brand perception. Companies carefully craft their messaging to create specific narratives about their products. Phrases like "sustainable" or "eco-friendly" can generate positive feelings, even when the reality doesn't live up to those ideals. How corporations frame their actions plays a crucial role in shaping public trust and loyalty, demonstrating just how much influence language has on consumer choices.

To be effective advocates for change, it's crucial to recognize the power of language. Being attentive to word choices and their implications can elevate conversations and promote more inclusive dialogues. We must acknowledge that the stories we tell and the language we use have tangible effects on the world around us. By understanding the importance of framing, we can enhance our skills as communicators and allies in the fight for social justice.

At the end of the day, the strength of language comes from its ability to shape our reality. By carefully considering how we share ideas and the words we choose, we can become more intentional in our discussions about social issues. This awareness empowers us to recognize the narratives we contribute to the public conversation and to engage in advocacy that reflects our values. In a world where language is always changing, the message is clear: let's harness the power of words to foster understanding, inspire action, and drive the societal change we want to see.

As we navigate the complexities of advocacy and activism, let's keep in mind that every word matters. The stories we share and promote have the potential to reshape how people think and motivate them to act. Language can unite or divide, empower or suppress, and it's our responsibility to use it wisely. By being thoughtful in how we communicate, we can help create a conversation that aligns with our shared values, advocates for justice, and ultimately moves society toward a more inclusive and fair future. The art of framing, when approached with care and intention, can become a powerful tool for those seeking to inspire change and challenge the status quo.

Chapter 4: Power Players—Who Moves the Window?

The Overton Window isn't just an idea; it's a lively interplay of influence, persuasion, and power that shapes how we talk about important issues. Grasping who moves this window—and how they do it—helps us understand how our social norms change over time. The key players in this game of influence can be divided into three main groups: politicians and leaders, activists and grassroots movements, and think tanks and intellectuals. Each of these groups has its own unique set of tools and tactics that add to the constantly changing landscape of public opinion.

Let's start with politicians and leaders. They often take center stage, using their platforms to sway public feelings and guide the agenda. These individuals aren't just figures of authority; they also represent change and are often seen as the gatekeepers of society's values. Their influence can feel almost magical, allowing ideas that once seemed out of reach to suddenly become part of the mainstream conversation. Take President Franklin D. Roosevelt, for example. When he introduced the "New Deal" during the Great Depression, he didn't just suggest new policies; he transformed how the nation thought about economic rescue. By presenting government intervention positively, he shifted the Overton Window to include ideas that once seemed extreme.

As we look deeper into political influence, we realize that not all leaders have the same weight. The environment where they operate significantly impacts their ability to bring about change. A charismatic leader can uplift an entire nation, while a less dynamic figure might struggle to make headway, even with solid ideas. This explains why some leaders can push fresh concepts into everyday conversation, while others fail to reach an audience. The discussion around climate change is a perfect example. Over the years, individuals like Al Gore and Greta Thunberg have played huge roles in changing how we view this issue. Their heartfelt appeals for action have not only raised awareness but also brought climate-related policies into public favor.

But the world of influence isn't limited to those in political roles. Activists and grassroots movements have also become powerful forces. They work from the ground up, rallying communities and building connections that go beyond traditional power structures. A classic example of this is the

Civil Rights Movement in the United States. Leaders like Martin Luther King Jr. and groups like the Student Nonviolent Coordinating Committee (SNCC) tapped into the power of collective action to challenge the status quo. Through peaceful protests, sit-ins, and boycotts, they brought issues of racial equality into the spotlight, effectively nudging the Overton Window toward justice and fairness.

Grassroots movements thrive on passion and determination. They often use creative strategies to engage the public, utilizing social media and digital platforms to spread their messages and reach audiences like never before. The Women's March on January 21, 2017, is a great example. Millions gathered in cities across the globe to champion women's rights and social justice, creating a wave of energy that highlighted issues like reproductive rights, gender equality, and sexual harassment. The sheer number of participants not only captured public attention but also significantly changed the conversation about women's rights in society.

On a different note, think tanks and intellectuals play a crucial role in shaping societal changes, adding complexity to the mix. These organizations often work behind the scenes, conducting research and producing data that inform policy decisions. Their work can help legitimize or challenge existing ideas, providing the intellectual backbone that supports political or grassroots efforts. Think tanks like the Brookings Institution and the Heritage Foundation, for instance, have influenced public policy discussions for years, each from its own viewpoint.

Their significance isn't just in the information they provide but also in how they frame issues. When we look at a topic like healthcare, the stories crafted by think tanks can profoundly affect public understanding of proposed changes. A report from a conservative think tank might raise doubts about a universal healthcare system, while a progressive group might spotlight successful models from other countries. These differing viewpoints shape public opinion and play a significant role in moving the Overton Window in various directions.

The interaction between these groups creates a lively environment where ideas are constantly negotiated and reshaped. This back-and-forth is often visible in the media, where narratives shift in real-time. For instance, the debate over immigration policy has changed notably in recent years. Politicians, activists, and think tanks have all played parts in shaping the story around immigration, with some presenting immigrants as essential contributors to society and others viewing them as threats. This multi-layered struggle for public perception shows how the Overton Window can shift dramatically in a short period.

The effectiveness of these power players in moving the Overton Window heavily depends on how well they adapt to their surroundings. The same message, delivered in different ways, can have wildly different impacts. Language, imagery, and timing are critical factors. A well-timed campaign that connects with the public's fears, hopes, and dreams can create momentum that changes societal norms and attitudes. For example, the compelling visual branding used by the Black Lives Matter movement has brought issues of systemic racism to the forefront, reshaping global conversations around policing and justice.

It's also crucial to understand that the influence of these power players isn't set in stone; it shifts as societal conditions change. The COVID-19 pandemic highlighted this reality, introducing a new wave of influencers and advocates. Public health officials became key figures, their expertise sought to navigate the crisis. Their ability to communicate clearly about the urgency of vaccinations, mask-wearing, and social distancing was pivotal in changing public attitudes toward the pandemic. This situation reminds us that anyone can rise as a power player when the moment calls for it, redefining who moves the Overton Window based on current needs.

Moreover, the roles of these power players often overlap and intersect. Politicians may borrow the language of activists to connect with grassroots efforts, while think tanks might team up with leaders to create effective policies. This collaboration can amplify their impact, driving more significant changes in public discourse. The #MeToo movement is a perfect illustration of this, where politicians, activists, and media figures came together to confront sexual harassment and assault, leading to widespread societal transformation. The outcome was a reshaping of the Overton Window surrounding gender-based violence, making discussions about consent and accountability part of everyday conversations.

At the core of understanding these power players is recognizing that their influence isn't just about the ideas they support but also the relationships they build. Forming coalitions and networks is essential for expanding their reach and effectiveness. Successful movements often thrive on teamwork, bringing diverse voices together to craft a narrative that resonates with a wide audience. This is where storytelling shines—narratives that humanize complex issues can break through indifference and inspire action.

Whether through social media campaigns, public demonstrations, or policy advocacy, the ability to shape the Overton Window lies in the hands of those willing to actively engage in societal conversations. It requires an understanding of the dynamics at play, along with the skill to express ideas in ways that connect with different audiences. In this sense, power players become not just shapers of discourse but also catalysts for change. By acknowledging their influence, we empower ourselves to take part in the discussions that define our society.

As we navigate this landscape, it's vital to stay alert and aware of the changes happening around us. The Overton Window isn't a fixed concept; it's a living reflection of our society's values, beliefs, and dreams. Understanding who moves this window—and how they do it—allows us to join the conversation and work toward a more fair and inclusive future. The power to influence social norms isn't just for a select few; it's a shared responsibility that calls for active participation from all of us. Together, we can join this dance of influence, helping to shift the Overton Window toward a vision of society that embodies fairness, justice, and compassion for everyone.

Activists and Grassroots Movements

While politicians can have a significant impact through their roles and decisions, the real heartbeat of society often comes from its activists and grassroots movements. These passionate individuals and groups become the voice of the people, challenging what's normal and advocating for real change right from the community level. With their relentless efforts, they connect with communities, raise awareness, and push the limits of what can be discussed—changing the conversation along the way.

To truly understand the influence of grassroots movements, we can look at the Black Lives Matter (BLM) movement. This movement has transformed how we discuss race and policing in America. It began with a strong desire to tackle systemic racism and police violence. Through grassroots organizing, social media, and public protests, BLM gathered support and demanded change. Key moments, like the protests following the tragic deaths of George Floyd and Breonna Taylor, not only highlighted the urgent need for police reform and racial justice but also inspired millions to join the fight against inequality.

The story of **BLM** started in 2013 when the hashtag #BlackLivesMatter popped up on social media after George Zimmerman was found not guilty for fatally shooting Trayvon Martin. What started as a simple hashtag quickly grew into a powerful movement, showing just how effective social media can be for organizing and rallying support. It allowed activists to connect, share their experiences, and plan actions on a scale never seen before.

Grassroots organizing shines because it lifts up marginalized voices, presenting issues in ways that resonate with many people. Through peaceful protests, marches, and community outreach, **BLM** has successfully pushed racial injustice into the national spotlight. The large scale of their demonstrations has caught the attention of politicians, the media, and the public, forcing them to confront uncomfortable truths about systemic racism and the deep-seated injustices in our society.

Key events, like the protests that erupted after George Floyd's murder in May 2020, highlighted how important this movement is. What began as a local response in Minneapolis exploded into a worldwide outcry against police brutality, with millions marching in unity all over the globe. Images of protesters holding signs saying "I Can't

Breathe" and "No Justice, No Peace" became symbols of a collective demand for change. This movement not only captured the nation's attention but also sparked discussions on policies around policing, criminal justice, and racial inequality. As public awareness grew, conversations started about defunding the police, redirecting resources to community services, and pushing for essential reforms to tackle systemic racism.

While **BLM** has made tremendous strides in raising awareness about racial justice, it has also faced obstacles like misinformation and backlash. Some critics have tried to label the movement as divisive or extreme, but this has only made its supporters more determined. Instead of giving up, activists have turned these challenges into opportunities to engage in dialogue and emphasize the movement's core message: justice and equality for everyone.

The impact of grassroots movements goes beyond racial justice; climate activism has also emerged as a powerful force shaping public conversations. Greta Thunberg, a Swedish teenager, has become a figurehead for the climate crisis, rallying young people around the world to demand urgent action on climate change. Her school strike for climate sparked a global movement, inspiring millions to take to the streets and call for policies that protect our planet.

Thunberg's activism shows how young voices can challenge traditional politics and environmental policies. Using social media, she has amplified her message and rallied supporters through global climate strikes. This grassroots approach has successfully expanded the conversation around climate action, turning what was once seen as a fringe issue into a mainstream concern that politicians can no longer ignore.

The climate movement highlights the power of youth engagement. Young people have emerged as key players in the fight for a sustainable future, creating a sense of urgency around climate change. The Fridays for Future movement, initiated by Thunberg, has seen students around the world walk out of classrooms, demanding action for climate justice. By confronting politicians directly and holding them accountable, these young activists have played a crucial role in reshaping the narrative around climate policy, making sustainability and climate justice vital topics in public discourse.

Both the BLM movement and climate activism show how grassroots organizing can lead to real change. These movements use various strategies that resonate with people's lived experiences, effectively framing their issues to attract a wider audience. Building coalitions has been key, as both movements have joined forces with other marginalized groups, amplifying their messages and creating a more inclusive narrative.

Additionally, social media plays a huge role in these movements. Platforms like Twitter, Instagram, and Facebook have become essential for activists to share information, organize events, and rally supporters. A catchy hashtag can spread rapidly, turning local events into global movements. The viral nature of these platforms allows for instant communication, keeping the momentum alive and making it easier to engage and mobilize large crowds.

However, while social media offers many advantages, it also has its downsides. Misinformation can spread just as quickly as the truth, leading to confusion and division. Activists must navigate this tricky landscape carefully, ensuring their messages are clear and accurate while also capturing attention. Balancing the urgency of their message with the complexities of the issues is an ongoing challenge that requires thoughtful communication.

Moreover, the complexity of grassroots movements means they often experience internal debates and disagreements. Different factions within a movement might focus on various parts of the broader cause, leading to differing strategies and goals. Yet, this variety of thought can also be a strength, allowing movements to adapt and refine their messages to resonate with a larger audience. The ongoing conversations and negotiations within these movements reflect the dynamic nature of social activism, where ideas develop and intersect.

The true power of activists and grassroots movements lies not only in the issues they fight for but also in the connections they build within their communities. These relationships create a sense of belonging and unity, nurturing a shared commitment to social change. Through community organizing, activists empower individuals to take charge of their stories, turning passive observers into active participants in the quest for justice.

The stories woven within these movements are crucial to their success. By sharing personal experiences and putting a human face on complex issues, activists forge connections that inspire empathy and understanding. The narratives that spring from grassroots movements resonate deeply, offering powerful counter-narratives to the often clinical and abstract language of policies and politics.

In this dance of activism, the role of empathy is vital. The ability to connect with others on a human level is essential for building coalitions and gaining widespread support for causes. When people feel seen and heard, they are more likely to engage and contribute to the movement. The art of storytelling becomes a transformative tool, allowing activists to frame their struggles in relatable ways that encourage action and solidarity.

Ultimately, the world of activism is always changing, adapting to new challenges and opportunities. As society evolves, so do the strategies used by activists. The COVID-19 pandemic, for example, highlighted the importance of virtual organizing and online advocacy when in-person gatherings were limited. Activists quickly adapted, using technology to hold online events, webinars, and discussions, ensuring their messages continued to resonate despite unprecedented obstacles.

The resilience of grassroots movements shows the strength of collective action. When people unite around a common cause, they can create waves of change that reach far beyond their neighborhoods. The fight for justice, equality, and sustainability is ongoing, and as the conversation continues to evolve, the role of activists and grassroots movements will remain vital in shaping public discourse.

By understanding the strategies and impacts of these movements, we can gain insight into the complexities of social change. Activists and grassroots movements are essential catalysts for transformation, reminding us that the power to influence public opinion rests in the hands of those willing to speak out, come together, and demand better. In this connected world, it's our shared responsibility to take part in these conversations, support meaningful causes, and work toward a future that embodies fairness, justice, and kindness for all. Together, we can create the change we wish to see, paving the way for a more equitable and just society.

Think Tanks and Intellectuals

In the rich world of public conversation, think tanks and intellectuals serve as the builders of ideas, working diligently to shape how society understands various issues. Often working behind the scenes, these organizations hold significant sway in guiding policy discussions and providing the knowledge that helps decision-makers navigate complex challenges. By examining the contributions of key think tanks, like the Brookings Institution and the Cato Institute, alongside the work of individual scholars and public intellectuals, we can grasp their deep influence on public opinion and policy.

First up is the Brookings Institution, one of the oldest and most respected think tanks in the United States, founded back in 1916. Brookings has earned a reputation for its thorough research and thoughtful analysis across many policy areas. Its scholars focus on urban policy, economic development, and foreign affairs, often sharing studies that shape the national conversation around critical issues. What makes Brookings stand out is its dedication to connecting academic research with real-world application, making its findings relevant to both policymakers and everyday citizens.

For instance, Brookings has been instrumental in shaping discussions around urban policy, especially when it comes to affordable housing and city development. As cities struggle with issues of affordability, Brookings researchers provide solid data and practical recommendations that help local governments and non-profits tackle these challenges. By showcasing evidence-based solutions to urban problems, Brookings not only influences local policies but also changes how people view possible solutions to pressing social issues.

In addition to urban policy, Brookings has made important contributions to discussions about economic development. Its analysis of income inequality, labor markets, and job creation has brought these issues to the forefront of national discussions. As lawmakers consider the growing divides among socioeconomic groups, Brookings' research provides insights that challenge traditional views and foster innovative thinking around economic policies. The ability of Brookings to break down complex economic topics into easily understandable ideas has been key to moving these discussions from the academic world to everyday political conversations.

Then we have the Cato Institute, which popped up in 1977 with a strong libertarian viewpoint. Cato's mission is all about promoting individual freedom, limited government, free markets, and peace. Its scholars challenge the norm, pushing back against government involvement in both economic and personal matters. What's really interesting about Cato is how it frames public discussions through the lens of personal liberty and a healthy skepticism of government power.

Cato has built a rich collection of research and analysis that has changed the way people talk about issues like taxation, regulation, and foreign relations. For example, its strong push for reducing government intervention in the economy highlights the problems and unintended results of excessive regulation, advocating for a free marketplace. This perspective has not only swayed public opinion but has also led lawmakers to reconsider certain regulatory practices. Cato successfully draws in a wide audience, from free-market economists to everyday citizens who care about personal freedom.

Cato also plays a key role in shaping conversations about civil liberties. Its research on topics like surveillance, drug policy reform, and criminal justice has introduced libertarian ideals into mainstream discussions, nudging public opinion toward a more individual-focused approach to governance. By emphasizing personal freedom and limiting government control, Cato has helped shift how we think about and address these important issues.

Beyond organizations like Brookings and Cato, individual thinkers and public scholars have also been crucial in shaping ideas and pushing the boundaries of what's seen as acceptable conversation. Figures such as Thomas Friedman, Noam Chomsky, and Yuval Noah Harari have offered their unique insights on various social issues, impacting both academic discussions and public understanding.

Friedman, known for his thoughts on global politics and economics, has a knack for connecting complex global matters with the general public. His bestselling books and frequent opinion pieces in major newspapers have made him a well-known figure, allowing him to influence narratives around globalization, technology, and climate change. By breaking down intricate concepts into relatable language, he empowers people to engage with important national and global issues, further shifting public perspectives.

On the flip side, Noam Chomsky has been a powerful voice in critiquing government actions and corporate influence in democracy. His analyses of media manipulation and propaganda have opened many people's eyes to how information is controlled and shaped, significantly changing how the public perceives media and its role in influencing opinions. Chomsky's work serves as a reminder that discussions about social and political matters are often guided by a few powerful groups, encouraging the public to question dominant narratives and seek out alternative viewpoints.

Then there's Yuval Noah Harari, whose explorations of humanity's future and the impact of technology on society have gained a lot of attention lately. His books, especially "Sapiens" and "Homo Deus," invite readers to think about the serious ethical questions surrounding our technological progress. By discussing these topics in an easy-to-understand way, he encourages more people to consider the futures we are building and the values they shape. His work pushes us to rethink how we view progress, ethics, and what it truly means to be human.

The relationship between think tanks, intellectuals, and public discourse is a complex dance that shapes how we talk about vital issues. These organizations and individuals exist within a larger ecosystem that includes media, politics, and public opinion. Each part interacts and influences the others, creating a continuous cycle that can either reinforce existing ideas or open the door to new perspectives.

As we watch how public opinion shifts, it becomes clear that intellectual engagement is a key part of making societal progress. Think tanks and public intellectuals not only provide research and frameworks for understanding complex issues but also act as sparks for change by challenging existing norms and encouraging open conversations. Their work often ignites discussions in the media, reaching far beyond academia into homes and communities across the nation.

So, how can we, as individuals, engage with these think tanks and intellectuals to help shape public discourse? One way is to actively participate in discussions—this could mean attending events, sharing their research with friends, or joining conversations online. By staying informed and speaking out about issues that matter to us, we can contribute to ongoing dialogues and help guide public opinion toward fairer and more inclusive perspectives.

Plus, supporting think tanks and intellectuals through donations or advocacy can help them continue their important work. In a time when misinformation can easily cloud our understanding, having strong, fact-based research is essential for building a more informed society. It's up to all of us to support the thinkers who challenge the norm and provide the frameworks necessary for grappling with the complexities of our world.

Ultimately, the work done by think tanks and intellectuals serves as a guiding light of reason and understanding in an often divided environment. They remind us that the journey for knowledge, while sometimes tough, is crucial to evolving our societal norms and policies. By engaging with their ideas, we can navigate the complexities of modern conversations and work toward a future that reflects our values and hopes.

Recognizing the value of intellectual engagement calls us to action. The flow of ideas, research, and public discourse is a dynamic force that can be harnessed to shape the direction of change in society. Whether through grassroots activism, informed discussions, or by supporting the efforts of think tanks and scholars, we can all play a role in shaping the narrative and advancing the conversation. The ability to influence public opinion is not just in the hands of the intellectual elite but also within each of us as we aim to create a more informed, compassionate, and just society.

Chapter 5: The Dark Side—Manipulation and Control

Propaganda Techniques

Propaganda often brings to mind grand speeches and eye-catching posters, but it's much more than just a political tool; it's a vital part of how we communicate. At its heart, propaganda aims to influence—it's an organized effort to change beliefs, attitudes, and behaviors among people. While the word itself can sound negative, suggesting manipulation and deceit, the truth is that propaganda is neutral. It can be used for good or ill, depending on who wields it and for what purpose.

Given how deeply propaganda has woven itself into history, it's crucial to grasp its various techniques. These strategies have been used by governments, businesses, and grassroots movements alike to sway public opinion. The methods in propaganda are wide-ranging, each tapping into our psychology and societal dynamics in different ways. Some of the most well-known techniques include bandwagon appeals, testimonials, scapegoating, and fear-mongering. Each one has its own unique impact, often playing on our emotions and biases to provoke specific reactions.

To understand just how powerful propaganda can be, let's take a trip back to World War II. This was a time when countries really harnessed propaganda to gain support for their causes. A famous example from the United States is the "Uncle Sam Wants You" campaign. This striking image of Uncle Sam, with his finger pointing right at the viewer, became a powerful symbol urging people to enlist in the military. The brilliance of this campaign wasn't just in its bold graphics; it also struck an emotional chord. The poster created a sense of urgency, suggesting that every able citizen had a duty to serve their country during such crucial times.

The bandwagon appeal is particularly relevant in this context. This technique operates on the idea that people are more likely to adopt a belief or behavior if they think others are doing the same. The "Uncle Sam Wants You" campaign cleverly gave the impression of widespread participation— everyone was joining the cause, and not doing so would mean standing apart from the patriotic crowd. This social pressure played a key role in shaping public sentiment during the war, tapping into our basic human desire to be part of something bigger.

When we look at testimonials in propaganda, we see how powerful personal stories and endorsements can be. People tend to trust the experiences of others more than abstract data or statistics. That's why you can find testimonials everywhere, from political campaigns to ads. Think about how much impact a famous actor endorsing a political candidate can have—people might think, "If this well-known person supports them, maybe I should too." This creates a strong link between credibility and popularity.

However, testimonials aren't just for celebrities. Ordinary people have also shared their stories to shed light on bigger issues. During the civil rights movement, for instance, activists told their personal experiences of discrimination and injustice, pushing the public to face some hard truths. These stories were powerful catalysts for change, showing how individual narratives can resonate deeply and inspire societal shifts.

Another effective propaganda technique is scapegoating, where a specific group or person is blamed for larger societal issues. This tactic has appeared throughout history across various cultures and political scenarios. Scapegoating offers a simple answer to complex problems by pointing out a clear "enemy" for people to rally against. During tough times, such as economic crises or social unrest, leaders often use scapegoating to distract from their shortcomings and gather support.

A notable example comes from the Nazi regime in Germany, which skillfully used scapegoating to amass power. They portrayed Jews and other marginalized groups as the source of Germany's economic troubles and societal decline. This kind of vilification not only stirred up hatred but also united people around a collective mission: to eliminate the perceived threat. The consequences of this propaganda were disastrous, leading to horrific violence and genocide.

Fast forward to today, and we can still see these techniques in action. Political campaigns are frequently filled with manipulation, as candidates use advanced advertising methods to influence voters. Social media has made this even more complicated; while it gives us more access to information, it also allows misinformation to spread rapidly.

Consider the term "fake news." This refers to the intentional spreading of false information that often pretends to be real news. Social media platforms can amplify this misinformation, making it easy for people to encounter and share misleading content. A notable example is the 2016 United States presidential election, during which false stories circulated widely, shaping voter perceptions and decisions. This highlights how modern propaganda techniques can be effective, underscoring the need for individuals to think critically and discern the truth in the information they consume.

Additionally, the bandwagon effect has found new life in our digital age. Hashtags and viral trends can create a sense of collective engagement, pushing people to align with popular opinions. The pressure to conform, magnified by the visibility of likes, shares, and retweets, can elevate certain narratives to the forefront of public conversation, regardless of their truth.

Looking at the past alongside the present, it's clear that propaganda techniques are not fixed; they change as technology and society evolve. The emotional appeals that were so effective during World War II are still relevant today, though they may take different forms. Just observe how marketing campaigns use nostalgia, fear, or excitement to sway consumer behavior. The same principles of persuasion apply, as advertisers tap into the psychology of their audience to drive sales and loyalty.

As we navigate this complex information landscape, it's important to be aware of these tactics and their broader implications. Recognizing when propaganda is at play is a crucial skill that empowers us to engage critically with the information we encounter. As members of a democratic society, we have a responsibility to question the narratives presented to us, examining the motivations and techniques that shape them.

By unpacking the intricacies of propaganda techniques, we reveal the forces that mold public opinion and influence our societal norms. From the emotional appeals of wartime campaigns to the digital echo chambers we see today, these strategies highlight the power dynamics at play in communication. Understanding these tactics isn't just for academics; it's vital for being an informed citizen in a time when misinformation can thrive unchecked. By encouraging critical thinking and responsible communication, we can better defend ourselves against the manipulative forces that continue to infiltrate our lives.

In the end, the insights gained from studying propaganda techniques call us to action. We need to recognize how these strategies work and actively challenge the narratives that attempt to limit our understanding of the world. By doing so, we can regain control over our beliefs and decisions, fostering discussions that prioritize truth, integrity, and inclusiveness.

Misinformation and Disinformation

The world we live in today is an overwhelming sea of information. Thanks to technology, especially the internet and social media, we're bombarded with news, opinions, and facts from countless sources. But amid this flood of information, a troubling reality lurks: the widespread presence of misinformation and disinformation, which have serious consequences for our communities, our health, and our understanding of what's real.

At first, you might think "misinformation" and "disinformation" are just two ways of saying the same thing, but they actually mean different things. Misinformation is false or misleading information shared without the intention to harm. It often comes from mistakes, misunderstandings, or the simple human habit of passing along information that isn't quite right. Disinformation, however, is much more dangerous. It's the intentional spread of false information meant to trick people. Knowing the difference is key, especially in a time when telling fact from fiction is harder than ever.

Let's take a look at the recent COVID-19 pandemic. The world found itself facing a new virus that changed everything we knew about our daily lives. As scientists hurried to figure out what was happening, misinformation started creeping into conversations. From wild theories about where the virus came from to unproven cures promoted by social media personalities, false stories spread rapidly. This was misinformation at its core—people sharing what they thought was true, even though it wasn't.

But in the midst of this chaos, disinformation lurked, deliberately planted by people with specific goals, both personal and political. False stories about vaccines emerged, aiming to create doubt and fear. The fallout from this was severe. Misinformation muddied the waters, while disinformation fed into conspiracy theories, eroding public trust in health organizations. As a result, vaccination rates declined, and communities faced outbreaks of diseases that were once under control.

To understand why people get caught up in these traps, we need to explore how our minds work. Cognitive biases play a big role in how we see information. For instance, confirmation bias leads us to seek out information that matches our beliefs and ignore anything that doesn't. This makes it easy for misinformation to take hold. When someone sees false information that aligns with what they already think, they're likely to accept it as truth, share it confidently, and help it spread.

Social media has made this situation even worse. The algorithms that prioritize engagement over accuracy create echo chambers where misinformation thrives. The more shocking or sensational a piece of content is, the more likely it is to be shared, regardless of whether it's true. By interacting with these platforms, people unknowingly contribute to an environment that rewards the spread of lies, pulling us deeper into misinformation.

The effects of this are serious. Consider the anti-vaccine movement that gained momentum during the pandemic. Supported by a mix of misinformation and disinformation, claims surfaced saying vaccines were unsafe, untested, or part of a government scheme. Despite overwhelming scientific evidence proving otherwise, these ideas took hold among some people. The real-world impact was staggering, leading to a rise in diseases like measles and mumps in areas where vaccination rates plummeted. The stakes in this fight against misinformation and disinformation couldn't be higher.

To protect ourselves in this age of information overload, we need to have the right tools to spot and fight misinformation. One of the best ways to do this is by verifying sources before deciding if something is credible. In our digital world, checking multiple sources has become a crucial skill. If an article makes a bold claim, it's wise to see if trustworthy sources back it up. Looking at different viewpoints not only broadens our understanding but also helps us separate fact from fiction.

However, checking sources is just one piece of the puzzle. Understanding cognitive biases can also help protect us against misinformation. The Dunning-Kruger effect, for instance, shows how people with limited knowledge often overestimate their understanding. This tendency to be overly confident can lead to the careless sharing of misinformation. By recognizing our own limits and staying humble, we can seek credible information instead of hastily passing along what we think we know.

Furthermore, educational programs aimed at improving media literacy can empower people to navigate the complex world of information. Schools and community organizations play a vital role in teaching critical thinking skills. By encouraging an environment where questioning and skepticism are welcomed, we can build a society that's more resistant to the allure of misinformation and disinformation.

The role of social media platforms in all of this is crucial. As major sources of information, these platforms need to take responsibility for what's shared through their channels. Many have started implementing fact-checking and moderation policies, but these efforts often struggle due to the sheer amount of information shared every day. Plus, algorithms that favor engagement over truth make it even tougher, amplifying false stories.

We need a team effort that includes tech companies, governments, and communities. It's important to ensure transparency in algorithms, promote accurate content, and create strong reporting systems for misinformation. Social media platforms should also invest in educational campaigns to raise awareness about misinformation and encourage responsible sharing among users.

It's also vital to connect with the emotions that often accompany misinformation. The power of storytelling can't be underestimated; stories that evoke strong feelings can cut through the noise and resonate with people. In our fight against misinformation, we should harness this power by sharing true stories that show the real impact of false narratives. Personal experiences that highlight the dangers of vaccine hesitancy, for example, can serve as powerful reminders of what's at stake in our battle against misinformation.

As we navigate this complicated landscape, creating a culture of openness and conversation is critical. Honest discussions about what truth means and why credible information matters can inspire people to take an active role in building a more informed society. By creating spaces where diverse viewpoints can exist together, we encourage a deeper understanding of complex issues, ultimately strengthening the foundation of our democracy.

The fight against misinformation and disinformation isn't just about getting the facts right; it's about protecting the very core of our society. As we face the challenges brought on by false narratives, it's crucial that we equip ourselves with the skills to tell truth from lies. By nurturing critical thinking, promoting media literacy, and engaging meaningfully with each other, we can work together towards a more informed and resilient society. These efforts affect not just our knowledge but also our health, our communities, and our shared future. In this information age, we have the responsibility to seek the truth, combat misinformation, and foster transparency, reminding ourselves that knowledge is truly power.

Ethical Implications

In a time when information flows abundantly, the ethical responsibilities of those who share it have become increasingly important. The ease of spreading content reveals not just the power of communication but also the moral questions that come with it. Persuasion, often seen as a vital skill in both our personal and professional lives, raises serious issues. Is it right to use manipulative techniques to persuade others, even if we believe our intentions are good? This question leads us into a deeper discussion about ethics, truth, and the bonds that connect us as a society.

To better understand this moral dilemma, we can look at ethical frameworks that have influenced human thought for centuries. Utilitarianism, which promotes actions that create the greatest happiness for the most people, often seems like a clear guideline. Yet, when applied to communication, it raises tough questions. For example, if a persuasive message encourages people to accept a beneficial idea—like a public health campaign—do we ignore how that message was delivered? If manipulative tactics were used to gain acceptance, can we really call the result ethically sound when the means were questionable?

On the other hand, Kantian ethics offers a different viewpoint. It stresses the importance of intentions and the inherent dignity of every individual, stating that people should be treated as ends in themselves, not just as tools to achieve a goal. From this perspective, any attempt to manipulate others damages their autonomy and dignity, no matter how positive the outcomes might seem. If communication turns into a tool for coercion, what does that say about the respect we show for one another? Examining these ethical approaches highlights the ongoing struggle between effective communication and ethical responsibility, pushing us to reflect on the meaning of our words and the motives behind them.

The fallout from unethical communication practices can be severe and widespread. History is filled with lessons from organizations and individuals who chose persuasion tactics that sacrificed transparency and integrity. Consider the notorious case of the tobacco industry. For many years, tobacco companies ran campaigns to downplay the health risks of smoking. Through misleading ads, selective data, and a cloud of scientific uncertainty, they convinced millions that smoking was an acceptable choice. Their goal was obvious: profit over public health. However, the results of this manipulation were devastating, leading to countless avoidable deaths and a whole generation of smokers who were misled.

Another striking example comes from the realm of political communication, especially during election seasons. The 2016 U.S. presidential election saw the rise of "fake news" and disinformation tactics designed to manipulate public opinion with dishonest narratives. Political groups and even foreign entities used social media to spread false information, targeting specific voter groups with tailor-made messages. The goal, often framed as political gain or ideological influence, led to increased division and a decline in trust in traditional news outlets. The long-term impacts of this manipulation are still being felt, as public discussions have become more fragmented, making it harder for citizens to engage in meaningful conversations based on shared truths.

As we think about these examples, it becomes evident that the ethical implications of communication go beyond the immediate effects of any single message. They ripple throughout society, influencing our collective understanding and trust in each other. Trust, once a foundation of healthy discussion, has been weakened by a culture that often values persuasive tactics over ethical behavior. This leads to a crucial question: how can we start rebuilding that trust?

Practicing ethical communication isn't just an idealistic notion; it's a practical necessity for creating a healthier flow of information. Each of us has a role in this ecosystem, whether we are consumers, creators, or curators of content. As individuals, we should develop the habit of reflecting critically on what we share. Before passing on information, we ought to ask ourselves: What is the source? What might happen if I share this message? Am I spreading misinformation, or am I acting as a responsible steward of accurate information?

Organizations, too, should make transparency a core value. In an era where public scrutiny is high, companies and institutions that prioritize honesty and accountability will not only build their credibility but also enhance public discussion. This means not only checking facts before sharing them but also being willing to admit and correct mistakes openly.

Educational efforts aimed at improving media literacy can empower individuals to navigate the complex information landscape wisely. By teaching people how to critically analyze sources and distinguish truth from manipulation, we can help create a society better equipped to resist the lure of misinformation. Programs that promote critical thinking and ethical reasoning can serve as vital resources, encouraging future generations to engage thoughtfully with information rather than simply consuming it passively.

We also need to think about the role of social media platforms and their ethical responsibility to foster honest communication. While these platforms have taken steps to combat misinformation through fact-checking and content moderation, the task remains daunting due to the vast amount of content generated each day. Companies must acknowledge their influence in shaping public discourse and take on the responsibility for the information shared on their sites. This includes developing algorithms that prioritize accuracy over sensationalism and creating easy ways for users to report misleading content.

At the core of ethical communication is the ability to connect sincerely with others. A strategy based on empathy rather than manipulation encourages real understanding and trust. Instead of resorting to fear-based messaging or sensational stories, communicators should focus on sharing true narratives that touch on an emotional level. These stories can be powerful tools for delivering important messages, making complicated issues more relatable and clear.

Building a culture of openness is incredibly important. We need to foster spaces for constructive dialogue, where various perspectives can coexist and engage meaningfully. Honest conversations about the nature of truth, the impact of misinformation, and the importance of ethical communication can motivate individuals to take an active role in shaping the information landscape. By creating an environment of curiosity and respect, we can work together toward a society that values transparency and accuracy.

Considering our roles in the information ecosystem is vital. Every message we share can either build trust or undermine it. As we navigate this intricate landscape, let's commit to being responsible communicators who value clarity, integrity, and empathy in our interactions. Promoting transparency and accuracy benefits not just us as individuals but also helps create a more informed and united society.

The ethical implications of communication are broad and intricate, involving not only the messages we send but also the values we uphold as a community. From personal exchanges to political discussions, our communication choices shape the world we live in, affecting public trust and societal dialogue. As we ponder the consequences of our words and actions, we need to strive for ethical practices that respect others' dignity and contribute to a healthier flow of information. By doing this, we not only enhance our own credibility but also join in the greater effort to build a society grounded in truth, understanding, and mutual respect. The path toward ethical communication is ongoing and requires both personal reflection and collective action, but the rewards—a more informed, engaged, and trusting society—are well worth the effort.

Winston Vane

Chapter 6: Overton in the Digital Age

Social Media's Amplification Effect

Social media has completely changed how we talk about important issues in our society. The days are long gone when a small group of editors and publishers decided whose opinions were worth sharing. Now, anyone with a smartphone or computer can share their thoughts and ideas with the entire world at the push of a button. This shift has opened up new ways of communicating, making it easier for everyone to share their views, hear different perspectives, and question the old rules that used to govern our conversations.

Think of social media as a megaphone for those who often go unheard. People and groups that struggled to get their messages across through traditional media can now join in on important discussions that were once out of reach. This change is especially significant for communities that have been overlooked in the past, giving them the chance to tell their stories, fight for change, and rally support in ways that wouldn't have been possible just a few decades ago.

One of the most fascinating parts of this amplification effect is how ideas go viral.

We might think that things go viral mainly because they're funny, have a celebrity behind them, or are shocking. While those factors do matter, there's a deeper reason. The key to an idea going viral often lies in how well it connects with people's emotions, reflects cultural trends, and is relevant to current issues. It's a careful balance of what the content is, the context it's shared in, and the timing of the message.

Take the #MeToo movement, for example. It burst onto the social media scene in late 2017. What started as a simple hashtag quickly turned into a worldwide conversation about sexual harassment and assault that had long been ignored. The timing was everything; it came at a moment when many people were ready to face uncomfortable truths about power and gender inequality. Thanks to social media, stories from survivors could be shared and validated in ways that crossed borders and broke down barriers.

The #MeToo movement is just one example, but it powerfully shows how social media can bring ideas into the spotlight. Similarly, movements like Black Lives Matter have made the most of platforms like Twitter and Instagram to shine a light on systemic racism and police violence. Videos showing acts of violence against Black individuals went viral, prompting millions to hit the streets, demanding justice. In these cases, social media acted as a spark, turning local incidents of injustice into a global outcry for change.

However, while social media can amplify the voices of those who have been marginalized, it also comes with some big challenges. The same features that allow information to spread quickly can lead to misinformation and divisive narratives. Because social media platforms often show users content based on what they engage with, echo chambers can form, reinforcing existing beliefs rather than challenging them. So, while social media can highlight different viewpoints, it can also create a split where opposing ideas struggle to be heard.

The nature of how ideas go viral also raises concerns about the longevity of movements that depend heavily on social media for visibility. The fast pace of online content can lead to what some call "slacktivism," where people think they're doing their part just by liking or sharing a post, rather than engaging in real action. This can water down serious social movements, reducing complex issues to quick, shareable snippets. In this environment, our challenge is not just to amplify voices but also to make sure that the conversations sparked by social media lead to real change.

To tackle these challenges, we need to focus on being intentional in digital activism. Successful movements that leverage social media often do so by creating spaces for genuine interaction and building connections that go beyond the screen. Organizations like the American Civil Liberties Union (ACLU) have recognized this need and use social media not just to spread information, but to rally supporters, organize events, and inspire active participation in the political arena. By tailoring their messages to resonate with the values and concerns of their audience, they can keep the momentum going and create real-world impact.

Social media's influence on the Overton Window is significant, changing how ideas are spread, debated, and accepted in society. As more people gain access to these platforms, the range of voices and experiences in public discussions keeps growing. Social media has become a mighty tool for changing narratives, challenging the status quo, and opening up conversations about topics that were once considered taboo.

But with this power comes responsibility. The ability to reach millions means we have an ethical duty to ensure that the information being shared is accurate, helpful, and constructive. As the digital world becomes more intricate, individuals and organizations must find a balance between the urge for virality and the commitment to fostering meaningful discussions.

It's clear that social media can amplify voices that challenge the existing norms. In a time when traditional gatekeepers no longer hold the power they once did, everyday people can make a significant impact. By exploring how social media amplifies voices, we can understand better how social norms can shift, how public opinion can change, and how the Overton Window evolves to meet the needs of our dynamic world.

As we witness the growth of digital activism and the strength of social media to rally people, it becomes increasingly important to engage with these platforms thoughtfully and critically. The chance to amplify voices, drive change, and challenge societal norms is available to anyone willing to dive into this complex and ever-changing landscape. By embracing what social media has to offer, we can use its power not just to lift up marginalized voices but also to pave the way for a more inclusive and fair future.

Algorithmic Echo Chambers

Navigating the world of social media can sometimes feel like stepping into a different universe, where our beliefs and opinions are magnified and reinforced. The algorithms driving these platforms are designed to grab our attention and keep us scrolling, playing a big part in shaping our online experiences. They create our feeds by presenting content that matches our interests, which leads to the creation of what we now call echo chambers. Inside these chambers, the sounds of our own beliefs drown out any opposing voices, isolating us in a comfortable bubble that can limit our understanding.

Echo chambers have been around long before social media, but the digital age has made them spread even faster. In the past, when we relied on traditional media, we might accidentally stumble across different viewpoints. Nowadays, algorithms are carefully crafted to track our behavior, learning what we like, what we click, and even how long we spend on each post. With this information, they tailor our feeds to reflect and often reinforce our existing views. While this might sound great—who wouldn't want a customized experience?—the truth is that it can create a harmful cycle that deepens divides and reduces our chances of encountering new ideas.

Take a look at political discussions on social media. Users are more likely to follow accounts that share their political beliefs, and the algorithms respond by promoting similar content. This creates a situation where opposing viewpoints aren't just ignored; they can completely disappear from our feeds. Essentially, we choose to shut out alternative perspectives and retreat into a digital fortress built on our own convictions. Consequently, the lively conversations once found in a more diverse media landscape become stunted, filled instead with a chorus of agreement, where differing opinions are not only unwelcome but often attacked.

A great example of this is the 2016 U.S. presidential election. Studies show that voters tended to interact more with content that aligned with their beliefs, which led them to encounter misinformation that further solidified those views. Social media feeds became bombarded with sensational headlines and polarizing content, creating an environment where users were constantly reassured about their stances. This dynamic resulted in a more divided electorate, where people viewed political opponents not just as individuals with different opinions but as enemies to be dismissed and vilified.

The effects of this polarization are serious. What happens online often spills over into real life, affecting how we communicate with each other, how we view policies, and how we understand complex social issues. When people become set in their beliefs, they're less likely to have open conversations or find common ground. This presents a major challenge for civic engagement; if we can't listen to one another, how can we work together to tackle important issues in our communities?

Additionally, echo chambers influence more than just political opinions. For instance, discussions around health, like vaccines or alternative medicine, can thrive in isolated environments, where individuals look for and share information that fits their existing beliefs. In these situations, well-meaning people might unintentionally spread false information, bolstering harmful narratives that can threaten public health efforts. Addressing these challenges is urgent; as long as echo chambers exist, misinformation will continue to thrive, creating discord and eroding trust in institutions.

While many point fingers at the platforms for this digital problem, it's critical to acknowledge our role in keeping these echo chambers alive. The choices we make about who we follow, what we share, and how we interact with different viewpoints all shape the digital landscape. Social media thrives on engagement, and when we reward content that confirms our biases, we unknowingly strengthen the very system that limits our exposure to a variety of ideas.

To navigate this complex digital world, we need to be more intentional. By actively seeking out different viewpoints and engaging with content that challenges our beliefs, we can start to break down the walls of our echo chambers. It takes effort—after all, it's much easier to scroll through a feed filled with things we agree with than to actively seek out dissenting opinions. Yet, the benefits of engaging with diverse perspectives are huge; not only do we gain a deeper understanding of complex issues, but we also cultivate empathy and develop a more nuanced view of the world.

This journey toward openness can take different forms. It might involve following people whose views differ from our own, joining online discussions that promote constructive debates, or connecting with organizations that value diverse opinions. By intentionally interacting with a broad range of ideas, we can challenge our biases and contribute to richer public conversations.

In this time of algorithm-driven content, awareness is our most valuable tool. We need to recognize the systems that shape our online experiences and understand how they influence our interactions and perceptions. By realizing that our digital world often reflects our own beliefs, we can take steps to break down the barriers that confine us. Engaging with diverse perspectives isn't just an intellectual exercise; it's a crucial part of being an informed and responsible member of society.

As we reflect on the consequences of echo chambers, it's clear that fostering healthy public discussion is a responsibility we all share—not just the platforms. We have the power to shape our digital experiences, to seek out voices that challenge us, and to engage in conversations that build understanding. By doing this, we contribute to a more inclusive and democratic dialogue that values differing viewpoints.

The digital age, with all its challenges and complexities, offers an incredible chance to connect with ideas. Social media can serve as a bridge for knowledge and growth, enabling us to learn from each other and broaden our horizons. However, this potential is only realized when we actively resist the tempting pull of easy confirmation and instead embrace the discomfort of engaging with new ideas.

Ultimately, fighting against echo chambers requires bravery, curiosity, and a desire to grow. By choosing not to remain isolated in our digital bunkers, we can work together to break the cycle of division and strive for a more informed and compassionate society. The challenge isn't about rejecting our beliefs but understanding that our view of the world can always be enriched by a variety of voices and experiences.

In the end, while the echo chambers we inhabit might feel cozy, they hinder our growth as individuals and as a society. It's crucial to be aware of the structures that support these chambers, to question the algorithms that shape our feeds, and to seek out the rich variety of human experiences that await just beyond them. By doing so, we can reclaim the narrative, promoting a culture of open dialogue that celebrates the diversity of perspectives while paving the way for meaningful change. The chance for greater understanding and collaboration is within our reach—if only we're willing to step outside our echo chambers and engage with the world in all its complexity.

Cyber Activism and Hacktivism

The internet has opened up exciting new ways for people to speak out and take action on social and political issues. No longer is activism just about gathering in a park with signs and chants; today, it can happen online, reaching people around the world in no time at all. Cyber activism and hacktivism are the names given to these modern forms of activism, using technology to challenge the status quo and hold those in power accountable.

At the core of cyber activism is social media, which has become a powerful platform for change. Websites like Twitter, Facebook, and Instagram are now the places where social change happens, allowing users to share their stories, rally support, and organize protests faster and more effectively than ever before. Trending hashtags can spark movements almost overnight, drawing attention to issues that might otherwise be overlooked. Whether it's the #MeToo movement bringing awareness to sexual harassment or #BlackLivesMatter fighting against systemic racism, these online campaigns have pushed important conversations into the spotlight, turning quiet complaints into loud calls for change.

A great example of cyber activism's impact is the Arab Spring, which started in late 2010. This wave of protests across the Arab world saw everyday people take to the streets to express their anger at oppressive governments. Social media played a key role in these protests, helping activists communicate, coordinate actions, and share information. People organized protests, documented human rights abuses, and rallied international support—all from their phones. The rapid sharing of images and videos showing state violence caught the world's attention and put pressure on governments to respond to the public's demands. The Arab Spring highlighted how technology can empower individuals, giving them a platform to demand change in ways that were once unthinkable.

Still, cyber activism has its hurdles. The digital world is full of misinformation, censorship, and surveillance. In many places, governments react to online protests by cracking down on free speech, passing laws that limit access to information and punishing those who dare to speak out. For activists, this creates a tricky situation; while social media can help organize movements, it also puts them under scrutiny and at risk. In authoritarian countries, expressing dissent online can lead to imprisonment or worse as the government seeks to silence any perceived threats to its control.

Hacktivism, a more aggressive side of cyber activism, adds another layer of complexity. Hacktivists use their technical skills to launch cyber attacks against those they see as unjust or corrupt. This can include defacing websites, leaking sensitive information, or disrupting services through denial-of-service attacks. Groups like Anonymous and LulzSec have made headlines for their bold actions against government agencies, corporations, and organizations they view as oppressors.

While hacktivism can shine a light on serious issues, it raises ethical questions too. The methods used by hacktivists can turn potential allies away, as their actions may come across as extreme or harmful. For instance, a denial-of-service attack might take down a website but could also hurt innocent users who rely on that service. Hacktivists face the challenge of balancing their desire for change with the possible fallout from their actions. Some believe that the ends justify the means, while others warn that such tactics can undermine grassroots movements' credibility.

One of the standout examples of hacktivism occurred in response to the 2010 WikiLeaks scandal, where sensitive documents revealing government actions were made public. Following this, a coalition of hacktivist groups targeted companies like PayPal and MasterCard, which had cut ties with WikiLeaks. By hitting back at these corporations, hackers aimed to disrupt their operations and highlight the dangers of censorship and corporate influence. This event underscored how hacktivism can act as a form of digital resistance, challenging the norm and advocating for transparency.

Furthermore, while social media amplifies voices, it can also put individuals at risk. The internet is a double-edged sword; it can be a space for dissent but also records every action. Once a tweet is sent or a post is shared, it can be hard to take it back. Activists must tread carefully, trying to use the internet effectively while keeping their privacy and safety intact. Many have turned to encryption tools and secure communication methods, but even these come with their own challenges.

For digital activism to truly make a difference, it needs to lead to real-world change. While online campaigns can raise awareness, turning that awareness into actual results is often tough. Social media can create urgency and foster discussions, but it doesn't guarantee policy changes or social reforms. Activists face many obstacles when trying to move from digital engagement to real action, including apathy and resistance from those in power.

The climate change movement provides a clear illustration of this point, with a surge of online activism in recent years. Groups like Fridays for Future have used social media to rally support for climate action, mobilizing millions of young people to take part in global climate strikes. While these efforts have successfully raised awareness and pressured policymakers, the ongoing challenge remains: how do we turn that awareness into lasting change? The fight for climate justice highlights a broader issue that many digital movements face: the need to maintain momentum despite systemic hurdles.

Another example comes from the struggle for LGBTQ+ rights, where digital activism has played a vital role in advancing issues like marriage equality and anti-discrimination protections. Online campaigns have created a sense of community and solidarity among people who might otherwise feel alone. However, as victories are celebrated, activists must stay alert to ensure that these rights are safeguarded and expanded. The digital realm can build connections, but it can also lead to complacency, where individuals feel they've done enough just by liking a post or sharing a video.

In this context, the Overton Window—the range of ideas considered acceptable in public discourse—becomes crucial. Digital activism can shift this window, bringing overlooked issues to the forefront and changing what is seen as acceptable or mainstream. When activists effectively use the internet, they can challenge prevailing narratives and advocate for social change in ways that resonate widely. However, if conversations stay limited to the online world, there's a real risk of disconnecting digital activism from its impact in the real world.

As we explore the landscape of cyber activism and hacktivism, it's important to recognize both the power and the risks that come with technology. The internet can connect people, allowing activists to gather support and organize actions on a scale never seen before. Yet, it's also a space where the stakes are high and the consequences of dissent can be severe. The fight for social justice in this digital age demands creativity, resilience, and a commitment to ethical values.

In the end, the challenge is to create a culture of engagement that prioritizes thoughtful activism over superficial gestures. Digital activism can wield incredible power, but it requires ongoing effort, teamwork, and a readiness to tackle tough conversations. Activists need to not only raise their voices but also listen to others, understanding that achieving social change is a group effort. In this interconnected world, every action—whether online or offline—plays a part in the larger story of progress.

Looking ahead, we must think about how to use technology responsibly and ethically in our pursuit of social justice. By navigating the complexities of the digital world with intention and care, we can tap into the strengths of cyber activism and hacktivism to help create a fairer, more inclusive society.

The fight for hearts, minds, and policies is ongoing, and the tools we choose to use will significantly shape the outcome. Embracing the potential of digital activism, while being mindful of its pitfalls, will be essential for fostering meaningful change in our increasingly connected world.

Chapter 7: Breaking Barriers—Activism and Social Change

Strategies for Effective Activism

Activism is often lively, urgent, and has the power to change the world. It represents the voices of those who won't settle for the way things are. These individuals believe that the world can be better—if they find the courage to demand it. But activism is more than just protests or signs. It's a complex effort that needs thoughtful planning, community participation, and the ability to adjust as society changes. When we think about what makes activism effective, we come across some key strategies that have stood the test of time and are crucial for driving social change today.

One of the most fundamental strategies in an activist's toolkit is grassroots organizing. This approach is the heartbeat of successful activism. It highlights the significance of local involvement and community action. There are many historical examples, but the Civil Rights Movement in the United States stands out. Leaders like Rosa Parks and Martin Luther King Jr., along with many others, used grassroots organizing to rally communities, raise awareness, and push for real change. Their work began in places like churches, community centers, and even living rooms, where discussions about equal rights, justice, and dignity took root.

Building a network of passionate individuals, nurturing relationships, and creating spaces for everyone to talk are all key parts of effective grassroots organizing. It's just as much about listening as it is about sharing your own ideas. Understanding the different voices and experiences in a community lays the foundation for coming together as a united force. For anyone interested in grassroots activism, try organizing small meetings that invite participation from all areas of the community. Create an atmosphere where everyone feels important and heard, and watch how individuals come together to become a powerful force for change.

As communities unite, the need for coalition-building becomes clear. No activist works alone; movements often grow from different groups coming together around shared objectives. The Women's March of 2017 is a perfect example of coalition-building, where people from various backgrounds, races, and beliefs came together to fight for gender equality and social justice. The strength of this coalition didn't just come from its size but from its commitment to inclusivity and shared values. Building trust among coalition members, encouraging open communication, and being willing to compromise are all crucial for keeping these alliances strong over time.

While coalition-building can be complex and involves many different elements, the benefits can be immense. By combining resources, skills, and networks, coalitions can amplify voices that might otherwise be overlooked. It's important to remember that while each group may have its own priorities, finding common ground is key to bringing diverse interests together. This unification can become a powerful tool in the ongoing fight for social change, not only leading to collaborative actions but also fostering a sense of solidarity that resonates far beyond immediate issues.

As we move beyond coalition-building, let's explore the structured world of advocacy campaigns. These campaigns are powerful tools for shaping public opinion and influencing policy. They are marked by clear messaging, targeted tactics, and a systematic approach to making change happen. Whether tackling climate change, LGBTQ+ rights, or racial justice, advocacy campaigns provide a clear path for activists aiming to create an impact.

Consider the environmental movement, which has effectively used advocacy campaigns to push for changes at local, national, and international levels. Campaigns like "Fridays for Future," inspired by Greta Thunberg's passionate activism, show how structured approaches can ignite a global movement for climate action. The success of these campaigns comes from their ability to craft messages that resonate with people, educate stakeholders, and inspire supporters to take action.

But advocacy isn't just about raising awareness. It also involves lobbying efforts directed at policymakers and public figures who can make changes happen. Advocacy campaigns should include plans for reaching out to these individuals, presenting clear demands, and building relationships that can ultimately lead to success in legislation. By using focused messaging, activists can shift public perceptions, making ideas that once seemed radical more acceptable to a wider audience.

In our digital age, we can't talk about effective activism without recognizing the major shift that digital platforms have created. Social media has transformed how activists connect, organize, and mobilize. Platforms like Twitter, Facebook, and Instagram have become essential for modern movements, allowing for quick mobilization and broad outreach. The Arab Spring is a powerful example of how social media can drive real-world action. It allowed citizens to share their stories, organize protests, and gather support both locally and globally, showing that the online world can lead to real change.

Similarly, the #MeToo movement demonstrated the power of social media as an activism tool. It sparked vital conversations about sexual harassment and assault, revealing the widespread injustices faced by many women in the workplace and beyond. Through hashtags and online campaigns, activists created a global dialogue about consent, power dynamics, and accountability. The strength of digital activism lies in its ability to connect people across distances, building a sense of global unity that crosses borders.

However, as activists navigate the digital landscape, it's crucial to remember that online efforts shouldn't replace in-person action. While social media is great for raising awareness, grassroots work in communities is what leads to lasting change. The real magic happens when digital mobilization works hand in hand with local engagement.

As you reflect on these strategies, think about which ones resonate with your values and the needs of your community. Effective activism isn't a one-size-fits-all approach; it's about recognizing the tools available to you and figuring out how they fit with your goals. As you assess your own activism toolkit, consider the methods that suit your community best and inspire your unique contributions to the broader movement for social change.

The journey of activism is about more than individual efforts; it's about working together, planning strategically, and being open to change. It's an ongoing conversation that needs everyone's participation, no matter their background or experience. As the world of social justice evolves, so must our understanding of how to break down barriers and create meaningful change. Embrace these strategies, connect with your community, and get ready to play an active role in the ongoing story of activism and social change.

Art, Culture, and Expression

On a chilly autumn evening, a group of artists gathered in a vacant lot in a lively urban neighborhood. The air was filled with a mix of excitement and nervousness as they prepared to unveil a massive protest art installation called "Voices Unbound." This impressive display featured hundreds of colorful fabric banners, each telling the personal stories of community members impacted by systemic injustice. As the sun set, casting warm orange and pink hues on the fabric, artists and local residents came together for a communal reading of the stories woven into the banners.

In that moment, something special took place. Strangers became friends, and a vibrant energy filled the air. As each story was read aloud, the crowd listened closely, their heartbeats syncing with the rhythm of the narratives. This blend of art and activism sparked a drive for change that resonated deeply within the community. The installation was not just a visual statement; it became a springboard for discussion, urging everyone to confront the uncomfortable truths about injustice and inequality that often hide in plain sight.

Art has an incredible ability to break down barriers and spark thought. It speaks to our hearts and challenges our minds, creating a space for voices that might otherwise go unheard. The blend of creativity and activism isn't just a modern trend; it has a rich history that mirrors the changing landscape of social movements. From the Harlem Renaissance, where artists like Langston Hughes and Zora Neale Hurston explored the complexities of African American identity and resilience, to the vibrant street art found in cities around the world today, art has consistently been a powerful tool for protest.

Think about the murals that brighten up worn walls in cities. These lively bursts of color often send messages that challenge oppressive systems. Street art, in particular, has become a strong voice for social commentary. Artists like Banksy and Shepard Fairey use their talents to highlight issues like war, consumerism, and environmental harm. Their work invites viewers to question societal norms and consider new perspectives. This form of art naturally engages the public in ways that traditional media often cannot, turning everyday spaces into places for conversation and reflection.

Throughout history, the arts have played a crucial role in activism across various cultural movements. Music, literature, and performance art have been especially impactful in shaping public awareness and rallying communities. The anti-apartheid movement in South Africa is a striking example of how music can unite and inspire. Artists like Miriam Makeba and Hugh Masekela used their songs to raise awareness about the injustices faced by their people, infusing their lyrics with a spirit of resistance. As their music traveled across borders, it created a sense of solidarity among those fighting for freedom, breaking down geographical and cultural barriers.

Literature has also been a powerful force for change. Writers such as James Baldwin and Maya Angelou crafted moving narratives that expressed the struggles of marginalized communities while promoting empathy and understanding. Baldwin's impactful essays on race in America pushed readers to confront the hard truths of systemic racism, while Angelou's autobiographical works celebrated the strength and resilience of Black women. Their literary legacies continue to inspire, providing insight and encouragement for those seeking to make a difference.

Performance art has also found its place in activism, inviting audiences to engage with urgent social issues in real time. Take the work of artists like Marina Abramović, whose performances challenge traditional ideas of art and identity, showcasing how art can provoke thought and dialogue. Whether addressing topics such as gender, race, or power dynamics, performance art invites viewers to become active participants, deepening their understanding of the complexities that surround social change.

As we look at the contributions of modern artists to activism, it's clear that the blend of art and social justice is alive and diverse. Banksy's street art is a great example of how creative expression can serve as a form of protest. His pieces—often infused with dark humor and sharp critique—address themes like war, poverty, and inequality. One of his most famous works, "Girl with a Balloon," shows a young girl letting go of a red heart-shaped balloon, symbolizing hope and loss. This image has evolved beyond its original context, becoming a global symbol of longing for a better world.

Artists involved in the Black Lives Matter movement have also harnessed the power of visual art to shed light on issues of racial injustice. Murals honoring victims of police violence have appeared in cities across the United States, transforming public spaces into memorials for those whose lives were tragically cut short. These powerful images not only pay tribute to the deceased but also remind us of the ongoing fight for equality and justice. Creating art in response to tragedy is both an act of mourning and a stand against injustice, reminding viewers that the struggle for justice is far from over.

The importance of storytelling in activism cannot be overlooked. Personal stories have the power to humanize issues and create empathy in ways that numbers and data often miss. When people share their experiences, they invite others into their world, helping to bridge gaps between different perspectives. This connection fosters understanding and unity, ultimately building a more compassionate society.

Activists are increasingly using platforms like social media to share their narratives, amplifying their voices in ways never thought possible. In a time when attention spans are short, storytelling has become a vital tool for engagement. Whether through videos, blog posts, or podcasts, personal stories can resonate deeply with audiences, inspiring them to take action for a common cause.

As we think about how art, culture, and expression intersect with activism, it's evident that creativity is a powerful engine for social change. The artists, musicians, and writers who challenge the status quo encourage others to reflect on their own experiences and engage with important social issues. Our call to action is not just to appreciate art for its beauty, but to see its potential as a spark for meaningful conversation and transformation.

Getting involved with art as a way to express activism can take many forms. Some might choose to join a local art collective, participate in community mural projects, or organize poetry readings focused on social justice topics. Others may find their voice through music, using songwriting to tackle personal and societal challenges. The possibilities are as varied as the individuals looking to express themselves creatively.

As you think about your role in this lively world of art and activism, consider how your unique talents can help create change. Creativity isn't just a solo journey; it thrives within a community. Working with others can boost your impact, weaving together diverse experiences and perspectives into a powerful story of resistance.

Art has a distinct ability to inspire, provoke, and unite us. It encourages us to question, listen, and engage with one another. Through creativity, we can deepen our understanding of the world, fostering empathy and solidarity across divides. In this time of social change, let's harness the power of artistic expression to shed light on the challenges we face and ignite the passions of those around us.

By embracing your creative talents and engaging with the arts, you can become an active participant in the ongoing conversation about social justice. Whether through visual art, music, literature, or performance, your contributions can reflect the struggles faced by many and serve as a symbol of hope for a fairer future. Together, let's celebrate the force of art and culture in our fight for a more just society. Through our shared creativity, we can amplify the voices that need to be heard and create a world where everyone can express themselves freely.

The Power of Young Voices

In the middle of a lively city, a new generation of activists is stepping up, their voices ringing out through the streets with an energy that's hard to miss. Imagine a scene filled with high school students, college kids, and young people from all walks of life coming together, holding bright signs and chanting in unison, driven by a shared purpose. In recent years, these rallies have become powerful symbols of hope and determination, shining a spotlight on youth activism. With a strong sense of urgency and fresh insights, these young voices aren't just repeating what's come before; they are leading the way for change, challenging the status quo, and calling for a better world.

One rally that perfectly captures this spirit happened a few years back when students from all over the country gathered in Washington, D.C. for the March for Our Lives. This event was sparked by the heartbreaking shooting at Marjory Stoneman Douglas High School in Parkland, Florida. It wasn't just another protest; it was a powerful show of unity that touched the hearts of many. The youth-led movement pushed for stricter gun control laws, an end to gun violence, and most importantly, a demand for their voices to be heard and respected.

As the young activists marched, you could feel their determination in the air. They waved signs with touching messages: "Enough is Enough," "Not One More," and "Protect Our Future." Each slogan expressed their fears and hopes for a safer world. The energy was contagious, as chants bounced off the grand marble pillars of the nation's capital. They weren't just speaking for themselves; they were voicing the concerns of those who couldn't. The rally marked a pivotal moment, not just in the fight against gun violence but in the broader movement of youth activism. It showcased the undeniable power that young voices can have when they unite for a common cause.

Youth activism isn't a new idea; history is filled with moments where young people have led the charge for social change. The Student Nonviolent Coordinating Committee (SNCC) emerged during the Civil Rights Movement, showing how young voices can spark significant shifts in societal attitudes. The students involved were often just teenagers or in their early twenties, fueled by a strong desire for justice and equality that pushed them to the forefront of the battle against racial segregation and discrimination. Their bravery and commitment played a crucial role in organizing sit-ins, marches, and voter registration drives, confronting deeply rooted systems of oppression in the American South.

There are many similar stories around the world that highlight youth movements sparking revolutions and reforms. The Arab Spring, started by young activists using social media, is another powerful example of how collective youth action can change political landscapes. These movements reveal a pattern: when young people are given a chance and the right tools to mobilize, they can effectively challenge injustice and bring about real change.

The unique insights that young people contribute to activism are invaluable. They often have a clear and honest view of the world, free from the cynicism that can come with age. With fresh perspectives, they question old norms and envision possibilities that might be overlooked by others. This spirit of inquiry is paired with a sense of urgency that prompts them to take action. Issues like climate change, gun violence, racial inequality, and economic unfairness aren't just abstract problems for these young activists; they are urgent threats to their futures. As they tackle these significant challenges, they do so with the unwavering belief that change is possible and essential.

Education plays a key role in shaping this activism. Schools and universities can be great places for nurturing critical thinking, encouraging civic engagement, and building leadership skills. Educational institutions have the potential to ignite a passion for social justice, empowering students to use their knowledge for meaningful change. When schools prioritize inclusivity and diverse perspectives, they create environments where young people feel encouraged to speak their minds, challenge injustices, and advocate for what they believe in.

This empowerment through education goes beyond the classroom. Community organizations and grassroots initiatives also play a vital role in equipping youth with the skills they need for activism. Programs that teach leadership, public speaking, and advocacy strategies help young individuals take charge of their stories. Mentorship from experienced activists can further strengthen this process, providing guidance and support as the next generation navigates the complexities of activism.

At the same time, the world of activism has changed dramatically in recent years, largely due to technology. Today's youth are digital natives, skilled at using social media platforms that allow them to connect, organize, and amplify their messages like never before. The power of platforms like Twitter, Instagram, and TikTok is enormous; they act as channels for quickly spreading information and mobilizing people.

These digital tools let young activists share their stories and viewpoints, sometimes going viral and attracting national attention. Take the #BlackLivesMatter movement, for example, which gained traction through social media, becoming a call for systemic change. Young activists have harnessed hashtags, powerful visuals, and engaging content to spread their messages far and wide. This connectivity creates a sense of unity among young people worldwide, enabling them to collaborate on campaigns that cross geographical boundaries.

However, this online landscape isn't without its challenges. Sometimes, online activism can slip into clicktivism, where people feel they have done enough simply by sharing a post instead of taking real action. The challenge lies in encouraging deeper engagement that goes beyond the screen. Digital literacy is crucial; young activists need to learn how to navigate social media thoughtfully, distinguishing credible information from misinformation. The ability to critically evaluate sources and engage in meaningful discussions becomes essential in our digital age.

Navigating the complexities of activism in this tech-savvy world requires a multi-dimensional approach. Young activists are not just passive consumers of information; they are also creators, storytellers, and organizers. They must learn to use digital platforms effectively while being aware of the limitations and challenges these tools can bring. This balance can be achieved through education that emphasizes critical thinking, responsible media use, and the importance of genuine engagement.

When we think about the role of youth in activism, it's clear that their voices are not only powerful but also essential. They offer fresh perspectives, challenge outdated ideas, and bring a sense of urgency to the issues that matter most. The energy and determination displayed by young activists can inspire others to join their cause and support their initiatives.

Supporting youth-led movements goes beyond just acknowledging their efforts; it calls for active participation and mentorship from older generations. Building bridges across different age groups is crucial to nurturing a sense of unity in the quest for justice. Experienced activists can share valuable wisdom, strategies, and guidance while also learning from the innovative ideas that younger generations bring to the conversation.

In many ways, the future of activism is resting on the shoulders of the youth. As they claim their place in the spotlight, they carry with them the dreams, hopes, and aspirations of a generation eager for change. Their bravery to speak out and demand justice serves as a wake-up call for all of us, reminding us that we all have a part to play in creating a fairer world.

The path to social change is rarely straightforward, and the road ahead will certainly have its challenges. Nevertheless, the resilience and determination shown by young activists prove that they are more than capable of overcoming these hurdles. They are not just inheritors of the fight for justice; they are active leaders, inspiring others to join them.

As we observe the incredible impact of youth in activism, it's worth thinking about how we can all contribute to this movement. Supporting their initiatives, providing mentorship, and amplifying their voices are key steps toward building a more just and inclusive society. The struggle for change requires a collective effort, and by standing with young activists, we honor their courage and strengthen the path to a brighter future.

In this moment of awakening, let's celebrate the power of young voices. Their passion, creativity, and determination remind us that the pursuit of justice is a journey we all share, regardless of age or experience. Together, we can uplift the next generation of activists, ensuring their messages resonate widely, sparking the flames of change in every corner of the globe.

Chapter 8: The Economics of Acceptability

The Corporate Influence on Policy

In our modern world, political power often goes hand in hand with economic strength, creating a scene where big companies can have a huge say in public policy. While democracy should mean that the voice of the people comes first, the truth is that large corporations often speak louder—largely because of their deep pockets. These companies involve themselves in lobbying, campaign contributions, and public relations to shape policies that benefit them. In this section, we'll look at how corporate interests shift the boundaries of acceptable ideas in our political discussions.

To grasp this issue, it's essential to understand just how much money goes into corporate lobbying. In the United States, billions of dollars are spent each year to influence lawmakers. A report from the Center for Responsive Politics, which monitors campaign finance, revealed that corporations and trade groups spent over $3.5 billion on lobbying in 2020 alone. This massive amount of money shows a serious effort to sway legislation, regulations, and public opinion. The financial power these corporations wield often decides which issues get attention and which voices are heard in politics.

A clear example of this influence is found in the tech industry. Giants like Google, Facebook, and Amazon have built up extensive lobbying operations to defend their interests. With ongoing debates about data privacy, antitrust laws, and taxes, these companies have been quick to create narratives that influence how the public sees their practices. For instance, when it comes to data privacy, rather than just defending themselves, they've worked to shape laws that protect their business models while pretending to care about consumer rights.

This manipulation highlights a key element of how corporate interests can shape what's acceptable in public discussion, often called the Overton Window. By persuading lawmakers to push through legislation that benefits them, corporations don't just react to public opinion; they actively work to redefine the ideas that are considered reasonable in the political sphere. Often, they create a sense of fear or uncertainty around proposed regulations, warning of dire economic consequences if their interests aren't safeguarded. This kind of framing can shift public sentiment, making once-radical proposals, like stricter data regulations, seem extreme or unrealistic.

Let's also consider how this plays out in environmental policy and the fight against climate change. For decades, fossil fuel companies have resisted climate initiatives, using lobbying to change public views on climate science. By questioning the scientific consensus and focusing on the economic risks of moving toward renewable energy, these companies have managed to distract from the urgent need for climate action. Their influence has broadened the Overton Window to include climate denial as a valid opinion, despite the overwhelming evidence against it.

The connection between corporate interests and political agendas doesn't stop at lobbying; campaign financing is another powerful tool in their arsenal. The vast amounts of money contributed by corporations and their political action committees (PACs) highlight their ability to sway decisions. Politicians who receive hefty donations from these entities often find themselves aligning with their interests, either consciously or subconsciously adjusting their policy views to keep that support coming. This creates a cycle: when politicians rely on corporate contributions, they push for policies that benefit those corporations, which leads to even more funding for their future campaigns.

The impact of this relationship is significant. Not only does it distort the democratic process, but it also silences the voices of everyday people. While corporations have the resources to lobby and sway opinions, individual citizens often feel powerless against such overwhelming financial power. This sense of disempowerment can breed apathy, leading people to believe that their opinions and needs don't matter in the grand scheme of politics.

Still, it's crucial to remember that the Overton Window can shift. Public opinion can change—sometimes in big ways—when grassroots movements rally together. The rise of movements like Black Lives Matter and the youth-led climate protests, led by figures such as Greta Thunberg, shows that when people come together, they can challenge corporate narratives and reshape what's considered acceptable in public discussion. Corporations, aware of this potential backlash, may change their tactics, attempting to align with these movements instead of outright opposing them.

Take the example of how companies have responded to climate change. In recent years, many corporations have launched sustainability efforts and promised to reduce their carbon emissions. At first glance, this seems like a positive step; however, it's important to look deeper into why they are making these changes. While some companies genuinely want to promote environmental sustainability, others may simply be trying to improve their public image to fit into the evolving Overton Window. By presenting themselves as eco-friendly, these corporations can reduce negative backlash while continuing their usual business practices, often without making any real changes.

The key takeaway is that while corporations can effectively shape policy and sway public opinion, they don't operate in a bubble. The dynamics of the Overton Window are complex, influenced by many factors. Movements that challenge the status quo create opportunities for dialogue and change, pushing even the most entrenched corporate interests to reconsider their positions.

In this intricate relationship between corporate power and public opinion, it's vital for individuals to stay alert and engaged. As citizens, we need to recognize the powerful role that corporations play in shaping policy and actively participate in conversations that influence the Overton Window. By pushing for transparency, demanding accountability, and supporting grassroots movements, we can help create an environment where a variety of voices are not just heard but are also essential in decision-making processes.

In a world where corporate influence is so widespread, it's up to each of us to critically examine the narratives we encounter. It's also important to remember that there are ways to confront the overwhelming power of corporate interests. Historically, citizens have come together to create change, whether through protests, boycotts, or simply making informed choices as consumers. These actions can collectively pressure companies to rethink their strategies and align more closely with the values of the public.

Understanding how corporations exert their influence is crucial for anyone who wants to take an active role in shaping policies that reflect fairness and justice. By being aware of the Overton Window and how it's manipulated, individuals can better navigate the political landscape and advocate for changes that match their ideals. In this way, we can work towards a more inclusive and representative democracy—one where the power of the individual isn't overshadowed by corporate interests but is instead harnessed to create a society that values the diverse perspectives and needs of its people.

Economic Crises as Catalysts

Certain moments in history stand out not just for what they immediately cause but for the deep changes they bring about in how society thinks and acts. Economic crises, in particular, have a unique power to shake up the beliefs we hold dear, reshaping our political landscape and often leading to significant, albeit sometimes controversial, changes. Events like the Great Depression in the 1930s and the financial collapse of 2008 remind us of how economic turmoil can challenge the way things are usually done and create space for new policies and ideas to flourish.

Let's take a closer look at the Great Depression. The economic crash that started in 1929 changed American life in ways that seemed unimaginable at the time. Before the crash, most leaders believed in a hands-off approach, thinking the market would fix itself. But as unemployment skyrocketed and banks failed, it became painfully clear that this belief couldn't handle the human suffering unfolding around them. Millions of Americans were left jobless and struggling, and in that dark time, ideas that once felt radical started to gain traction.

One of the most important shifts during this period was the acceptance of John Maynard Keynes' economic theories. Keynes suggested that the government should step in to help the economy when times got tough. His ideas went against the grain of traditional economic thinking, but the desperation of the era made people more open to them. This led to the creation of the New Deal, which introduced a variety of social safety nets that changed the relationship between the government and the American people forever. Programs like Social Security and unemployment insurance helped redefine our social contract, paving the way for a more active role for the government in economic matters.

Personal stories from that time vividly illustrate the blend of despair and hope that people felt. Imagine a family struggling to get by, with the father losing his job when the factory he worked at closed down due to a lack of demand. Once a comfortable middle-class family, they now found themselves seeking help from the government— something that would have seemed unimaginable just a few years earlier. As they witnessed their neighbors facing the same hardships, they developed a shared understanding: the old ways just weren't working anymore, and change was necessary.

Now, let's jump ahead to the 2008 financial crisis, which brought its own set of challenges and revelations. The fall of major financial institutions sent shockwaves around the world, and as people lost their homes and watched their savings disappear, a new conversation began to take shape. The largely unregulated financial sector suddenly became a target of public anger. Frustration boiled over into grassroots movements like Occupy Wall Street, which echoed the feelings of a generation disillusioned by the excesses of capitalism.

In the wake of this crisis, discussions about income inequality and corporate greed gained significant traction. People took to the streets, demanding that the institutions responsible for their financial hardships be held accountable. This movement shifted the conversation around capitalism, forcing a critical look at the power dynamics that had been allowed to thrive for too long. This change wasn't just a reaction to the economic downturn; it signified a broader awakening about how wealth and political power intersect.

Stories from people affected during this time highlight the deep frustration many felt. One single mother, who lost her home to foreclosure, spoke about the betrayal she felt from a system that prioritized bailing out corporations over supporting everyday people. Her experience resonated with countless others, creating a strong narrative that called for systemic change. Although the crisis was heartbreaking, it sparked a drive for new conversations about economic policy, challenging long-held beliefs about the stability of financial institutions and the fairness of capitalism.

The changes brought on by these crises come not just from economic despair but also from the hard work of grassroots organizations and community efforts. During the Great Depression, labor unions and advocacy groups rallied people around the need for reform, creating a chorus of voices that demanded change. These movements fought for workers' rights, better pay, and improved working conditions, ultimately influencing public policy. They helped bring ideas that were once considered extreme into the mainstream conversation.

In a similar way, after the 2008 crisis, groups like Occupy Wall Street and other movements focused on economic justice rallied everyday citizens, challenging the narratives promoted by corporate interests. These organizations showed that collective action could take on the established order, sparking discussions around accountability for Wall Street, tax reforms, and the need for wealth redistribution. The idea that questioning the norms of capitalism was not just acceptable but necessary became a rallying cry for a generation eager to reshape the economic landscape.

While crises can lead to significant change, they also highlight the delicate nature of societal norms. The acceptance of progressive policies during tough times often hangs by a thread, depending on the public's ability to organize and maintain momentum for change. The Great Depression resulted in the establishment of safety nets that have lasted for decades, but these same programs have faced challenges over the years, especially during economic recoveries when the urgency for reform fades.

Looking back, the lessons from the 2008 financial crisis feel particularly relevant as we face new economic realities today. The conversations about income inequality, corporate influence, and the need for regulatory reform are just as important now as they were then. The movements that arose in response to that crisis are still resilient, but the fight to make new ideas accepted continues. Each economic downturn serves as both a warning and an opportunity—a chance to rethink our values and priorities and to stand up against entrenched interests, advocating for a fairer society.

As we face the complexities of today's economic challenges, it's vital to stay engaged and aware. Economic crises, while painful, should not just be seen as moments of despair; instead, they represent crucial times when we can rethink and reshape our values. The experiences of those who have faced these hardships remind us of the strength that comes from working together and the importance of questioning the norms that govern our lives.

The message is clear: history has shown us that economic crises can act as triggers for meaningful change, pushing us to reconsider the ideas and policies that impact our lives. Understanding this connection empowers individuals and communities to seize the chance for transformation in the face of adversity, recognizing that every challenge carries the potential for a more just and equitable future. By staying actively involved, we can help guide the conversation towards inclusive solutions that reflect the diverse needs and dreams of our society.

Globalization and Trade

Globalization is a powerful force that has changed the way we think about trade and commerce. This phenomenon has created a world where different economies, cultures, and societies are closely connected. It has reshaped how we exchange goods and services across borders and changed how people view and engage with economic matters. As we move toward a more connected world, the Overton Window—the range of ideas that people see as acceptable—has expanded, giving space for voices that were previously overlooked to join the conversation about trade agreements and what they mean for everyone.

To truly understand globalization and trade, it's essential to recognize the two forces at play: opportunity and challenge. In wealthier countries, globalization often means access to bigger markets, lower costs of production, and a wider variety of goods for consumers. However, the story is more complicated for developing nations. While globalization can lead to growth and investment, it can also put local jobs and traditions at risk. This push and pull can shift public opinions, reflecting changes in the economic landscape and how people feel about these shifts.

A prime example of this is the North American Free Trade Agreement (NAFTA), which started in 1994. When it was first introduced, many supporters viewed it as a significant step toward free trade, promising job creation and economic prosperity for North America. However, the effects were more mixed. While some sectors thrived, others, especially in manufacturing, faced serious challenges as companies moved production to Mexico to take advantage of lower wages. This sparked a strong backlash, particularly from labor unions and environmental groups, who argued that NAFTA favored large corporations over workers and the planet. This discontent highlighted a growing divide in public opinion, reflecting a broader anxiety about the rapid pace of globalization.

The rise of social movements against trade agreements like NAFTA was more than just a reaction to economic changes; it was a rallying cry for those who felt left behind by the global economy. Labor unions fought to protect jobs, while environmental activists brought attention to the environmental harm caused by increased trade. This shift in sentiment led to more discussions about fair trade practices, sustainability, and workers' rights. The conversation around trade agreements transformed from a strictly economic focus to include social and environmental concerns.

A similar situation unfolded with the Trans-Pacific Partnership (TPP), which aimed to unite twelve countries in the Pacific Rim under one trade agreement. Advocates believed this would boost economic growth and help counter China's influence in the region. But as negotiations progressed, public opinion began to shift, raising concerns about potential damage to labor rights and environmental protections, along with a lack of transparency in the talks. The backlash against the TPP showed how aware the public had become, questioning not just the economic benefits of such deals but also their wider impact on society.

To bring this to life, imagine a factory worker in the Midwest whose future was turned upside down by changing trade policies. For years, he felt proud of his work, knowing he was part of an industry that supported many families. But when his company decided to move production overseas to cut costs, the once-busy factory floor became eerily quiet. Suddenly, he found himself without a job, benefits, or financial security, turning him into another statistic affected by globalization. His frustration and sense of betrayal resonated throughout his community, where neighbors who once felt secure now faced uncertainty.

Stories like this remind us that the effects of globalization aren't just about numbers and statistics; they're about real people and their experiences. Workers, who were often ignored in discussions about trade agreements, are now speaking out, making sure their voices and concerns are part of the conversation. It's clear that we need to listen to everyone involved in this dialogue, making sure that the perspectives of all stakeholders are considered as we discuss globalization and trade.

The global economy also raises important questions about national sovereignty and whether protectionist policies are acceptable. As countries become more intertwined through trade agreements, finding the right balance between protecting local industries and embracing the benefits of global trade becomes a delicate task. In some cases, public opinion may lean toward protectionism as people seek to defend their jobs from the challenges of globalization. This highlights how the Overton Window can shift, with ideas that once seemed extreme—like pulling out of trade agreements or increasing tariffs—becoming more acceptable in public discussions.

The environment of globalization is further complicated by the blend of economic and political realities. As governments face public dissatisfaction with trade policies, they often find themselves in a tight spot. They must balance the demands of a global economy that calls for openness and competitiveness with the need to respond to the concerns of citizens worried about job security and cultural identity in the face of foreign competition. This tension creates a battleground for trade policies, where the deeper implications of globalization are debated, and the Overton Window continues to change.

While global markets offer clear opportunities, they also come with risks that we cannot ignore. Understanding these dynamics is crucial. Policymakers need to ensure that the rewards of globalization are shared fairly, so no group is left out. This means approaching trade agreements with a focus on inclusivity and responsiveness to the needs of those most impacted.

As we navigate the challenges of globalization, it's vital for individuals and communities to join this discussion with an open mind. The complexities of trade and its impact on society require a collective effort to support policies that emphasize fairness, sustainability, and social responsibility. The conversation around globalization and trade is always evolving, and as people's attitudes change, so should the frameworks that guide economic engagement.

In the end, moving toward a fairer global economy relies on understanding the interplay of ideas, experiences, and voices that shape public conversations. By sharing the stories of those affected by globalization and trade policies, we create a fuller picture of the many factors that influence the Overton Window. This empowers us to advocate for changes that mirror the values and dreams of a diverse society.

The call for inclusive dialogue is more than just a suggestion; it's a recognition that while globalization poses challenges, it also holds the potential to create a more connected and just world. As we engage with the complexities of the global economy, we must remain open to understanding the wide range of perspectives that contribute to shaping our shared future. The stories of workers, communities, and advocates cross borders, reminding us that in the broad story of globalization, every voice counts, and every experience is a vital part of the larger conversation.

Chapter 9: Personal Windows—Applying the Concept to Everyday Life

The Power of Self-Awareness

There's a huge difference between just going through the motions of life and truly engaging with the world around us. This difference matters a lot when we think about the Overton Window, which is all about how public opinion shifts and what ideas become acceptable to discuss. Self-awareness is like a pair of glasses that helps us see our own beliefs and biases more clearly. It helps us realize how our personal views shape our interactions and influence what our communities think.

Being self-aware means shining a light on the hidden corners of our thoughts and motivations. It encourages us to ask hard questions: Why do I believe what I do? Are these my thoughts, or am I just repeating what society tells me? These questions can lead us on a path of personal discovery that makes it easier for us to have meaningful conversations. This journey takes courage because it means facing the uncomfortable truths about our own biases. But the benefits we gain are well worth it.

Picture a conversation at a dinner party where a hot-button topic comes up—

maybe it's climate change, social justice, or immigration. The views around the table might be all over the place. Some people speak passionately, while others are quiet or hesitant, fearing they'll be shut down. In moments like this, self-awareness can act like a bridge. It helps us manage our emotional reactions and express our thoughts more clearly. Instead of jumping to defend our position, a self-aware person might take a moment to reflect and respond with understanding rather than fear.

Noticing how we react to different opinions is really important. Do we feel like arguing, shutting down the discussion, or leaning in to listen? Self-awareness helps us recognize these feelings and choose how we want to engage. This way, we can shift from being passive observers to active participants in the conversations that shape our world.

Moreover, self-awareness cultivates empathy. When we acknowledge our biases and understand where our beliefs come from, we become more open to seeing things from other people's perspectives. This compassionate approach can lead to conversations that might otherwise turn into conflicts. By recognizing that different views have value, we open the door for discussions that honor the messy complexity of human experiences. It's through this shared understanding that we can start to widen the Overton Window, allowing a greater variety of views and ideas to come forth.

Think about major historical movements that sparked real change. Take the civil rights movement as an example; it wasn't just about protests and speeches. It was a powerful awakening of society's consciousness. Leaders like Martin Luther King Jr. recognized the importance of self-awareness. They understood the biases that existed in society and dedicated their lives to changing public opinion. Their ability to share a vision of equality and justice shifted the Overton Window, making ideas that once seemed extreme acceptable in the mainstream.

We can learn a lot from these examples in our own lives. Each of us has the power to impact our social circles, whether that involves discussing tough topics with family and friends or pushing for change in our workplaces. The key is being willing to be self-aware and approaching conversations with curiosity instead of judgment.

To grow in self-awareness, it helps to develop personal practices that encourage reflection. Keeping a journal, practicing mindfulness, or talking with trusted friends can all deepen our understanding of our beliefs and how they affect our interactions.

These habits can help us spot patterns in our thinking and behavior that might be holding us back from connecting with others.

Self-awareness isn't a one-time thing; it's an ongoing journey. As society changes, we need to keep updating our understanding of ourselves. We owe it to ourselves and our communities to regularly reflect on our beliefs, question our assumptions, and stay open to new ideas. When we view the world through this lens, we not only enrich our own lives but also contribute to a broader discussion that can shift the Overton Window.

Our personal journeys toward self-awareness can create ripples that affect those around us. Imagine a situation at work when a colleague shares a controversial view. Instead of dismissing it immediately, practicing self-awareness might look like taking a moment to consider why that opinion stirs a strong reaction in us. Is it based on personal experiences, fear, or maybe a misunderstanding? This kind of reflection can lead to a more thoughtful conversation, one that encourages understanding instead of conflict.

In a time when society can feel divided over many issues, growing our self-awareness can be a powerful way to bridge those gaps. It helps break down the walls built by fear and misunderstanding. As we engage with our own beliefs, we can challenge the status quo and advocate for ideas that might have once felt too radical or unacceptable. Finding the courage to express our thoughts, rooted in self-awareness, can lead to significant changes in how we interact with the world.

The journey of self-awareness is deeply personal but also interconnected. Each person's growth can help spark a larger cultural change, inviting others to join the conversation. By sharing our experiences and perspectives, we open doors for collective understanding, which ultimately helps expand the Overton Window. When we start to recognize our biases and limitations, we empower ourselves to share that understanding with others, fostering a culture of dialogue and respect.

As we explore the ins and outs of the Overton Window in our daily lives, let's keep in mind that the power to influence social norms starts with us. By nurturing self-awareness, we can become agents of change, pushing the boundaries of what's accepted and helping shape a more inclusive and fair future. The path might be challenging, but it's also filled with opportunities for growth.

Every conversation we engage in presents a chance. A chance to listen, learn, and grow. When we approach each interaction with self-awareness and empathy, we create an atmosphere that encourages open dialogue. This not only leads to personal growth but also sparks a collective awakening. If we can connect with one another from a place of understanding, we can gradually shift public opinion. Ultimately, it's this shared awareness that holds the key to building a more inclusive society where diverse perspectives are celebrated.

The journey of self-awareness isn't just an individual quest; it's something we do together. As we shine a light on our own biases and beliefs, we open up paths for others to do the same. In this way, we contribute to a culture of openness, dialogue, and transformation. In each moment, we hold the power to influence not just ourselves, but our communities, institutions, and society as a whole. And it all starts from within.

Communication Across Divides

In a world buzzing with social media and instant messaging, it's quite ironic that even though we're more connected than ever, our conversations often feel shallow and filled with misunderstandings. It seems we've gotten really good at sharing our thoughts, but not so great at really communicating with each other. The deep divides we see in society today highlight just how important it is to improve our communication skills. To really connect and mend those divides, we need more than just the exchange of information; we need to create conversations built on empathy that foster real understanding, especially when discussing tricky topics.

When we picture conversations across divides, a lively scene comes to mind—lots of passionate voices, raised eyebrows, and maybe even a few frustrated sighs. Think about a family dinner where political opinions clash like heavyweight fighters, or a community meeting where differing views on local projects spark intense debates. These moments, charged with emotion, can easily spiral into shouting matches or, even worse, awkward silence as people retreat to their corners. But hidden within these discussions is the potential for true connection. It's vital to see that dialogue isn't just a contest of cleverness or a chance for self-expression. Instead, it's a wonderful opportunity to explore the richness of different viewpoints—a moment to listen and be truly heard.

One approach that stands out for moving past surface-level chats is empathetic listening. This isn't just about hearing words being spoken; it's about genuinely engaging with another person's perspective. Think about sitting across from someone whose opinions are completely different from yours. Instead of getting ready to counter their points while they're talking, you lean in, fully absorbing their words. You listen not just to reply, but to really understand. This is empathetic listening—a skill that takes practice and focus but brings about deeper, more meaningful conversations.

Empathetic listening is grounded in the idea that everyone brings their own unique experiences, beliefs, and emotions into a conversation. Recognizing this allows for a richer connection. When we practice empathetic listening, we put our judgments on hold, allowing us to appreciate the complexity of someone else's viewpoint. This doesn't mean we have to agree with them; it simply means we're open to understanding their perspective.

To build this skill, we can use some straightforward techniques. For example, summarizing what the other person has shared can be a powerful way to show you're trying to understand. If a friend is expressing their worries about environmental policies, you might say, "So, if I understand you correctly, you feel that the current rules aren't doing enough to fight climate change, and that worries you for future generations." This technique not only validates their feelings but also encourages more in-depth exploration of their thoughts.

Another helpful strategy is to ask open-ended questions. Instead of asking, "Do you think this policy works?" try asking, "What do you see as the strengths and weaknesses of this policy?" These kinds of questions encourage deeper discussions and can uncover layers of thought and emotion that a simple yes or no wouldn't touch. This approach helps create richer conversations, allowing both people to explore and understand the complexities of each other's viewpoints.

While empathetic listening is an incredibly valuable skill, it can be tough to apply, especially in heated discussions. It's easy to slip into defensiveness or dismissiveness when faced with opposing viewpoints. Let's consider a scenario many of us have encountered.

Imagine being in a work meeting where a colleague shares a bold idea for a project. You've spent months perfecting a different approach that you believe is much better. Instead of seeing this as a chance for discussion, your stomach tightens with frustration. Your heart races, and your mind spins with counterarguments. This is a common trap—defensiveness can shut down productive conversation, blocking the flow of ideas and preventing true understanding.

Now, let's flip that scenario on its head. What if, instead of jumping in with your own thoughts right away, you took a moment to ask questions? "What inspired this idea? What parts do you think would resonate with our clients?" By shifting your focus from response to inquiry, you not only show respect for their input but also open the door to collaboration. This small adjustment can turn a potentially tense exchange into a constructive conversation.

As we reflect on how we communicate, it's crucial to notice patterns that might get in the way of productive discussions. Do we often interrupt others? Are we quick to label their opinions as 'wrong' or 'misguided'? These habits can build walls between us rather than helping us connect. Being aware of how we respond to different opinions can lead us to tweak our communication styles, making it easier to have more constructive dialogues.

Look at the strong impact of respectful communication seen in various community organizations and social movements. Programs aimed at bridging divides in polarized communities often focus on creating safe spaces for conversations, where people can share their views without fear of being judged. Through guided dialogues, participants learn to listen and speak with empathy.

A great example is the organization Better Angels, which brings people with opposing political views together for constructive talks about their beliefs. Participants often come from different backgrounds and hold vastly differing opinions, yet through structured dialogues, they learn to listen actively and share their thoughts respectfully. The results of these conversations can be life-changing; people frequently leave with a deeper understanding of their counterparts and their motivations.

Moreover, the benefits of empathetic listening go beyond individual talks; it can spark broader changes in society. Think back to the civil rights movement, where leaders used dialogue and understanding to reach audiences who might be resistant to change. Martin Luther King Jr. and others understood that building empathy was crucial for changing public opinion on racial justice. They worked to engage not just their supporters but also those who disagreed with them, showing how effective communication can lead to significant social change.

As we navigate our own conversations, we can draw inspiration from these examples to foster a culture of empathy and respect. Each of us has the power to influence our surroundings. Whether it's tackling tough topics with family or participating in community activism, the principles of empathetic listening can guide our interactions.

Imagine a community meeting where locals come together to discuss a proposed development project. Opinions can vary widely—from strong opposition to enthusiastic support. Instead of letting the conversation break down into chaos, the facilitator encourages everyone to practice empathetic listening. By summarizing each viewpoint and asking open-ended questions, the tone shifts from conflict to teamwork. As residents begin to grasp each other's concerns and hopes, a shared vision emerges, building a sense of community that goes beyond individual differences.

To sharpen our empathetic communication skills, we can weave some ongoing practices into our daily lives. Taking regular time for reflection—whether through journaling or mindfulness—helps us explore our feelings and reactions to differing opinions. This practice deepens our awareness of our biases, boosting our capacity to empathize with others.

Additionally, engaging in role-playing scenarios with friends or colleagues can offer a safe space to practice empathetic listening. By simulating challenging conversations, we can explore various responses and refine our techniques. This practice not only boosts our comfort level but also prepares us for real-world discussions with grace and understanding.

As we dive into the art of communication, let's remember that every conversation is a chance—not just to share our thoughts but to connect, learn, and grow. When we approach discussions with empathy and a sincere desire to understand, we create an environment that promotes openness and respect. This atmosphere benefits not only ourselves but also society as a whole, as it lays the groundwork for a more inclusive and collaborative community.

In this journey toward effective communication, we need to recognize that the road may have its bumps. There will be moments of frustration and confusion. However, committing to empathetic listening can help us navigate these challenges with resilience and grace. By nurturing a culture of understanding, we can gradually change the way we talk about difficult topics, transforming them from battlegrounds into spaces for teamwork and growth.

In our interconnected world, being able to communicate effectively across divides is not just a valuable skill; it's an essential one. As we learn to engage with each other empathetically, we not only enrich our own lives but also contribute to a greater understanding in society. The conversations we have can serve as bridges, creating connections that go beyond our differences.

Ultimately, our aim isn't simply to convince others of our views; it's to create a sense of respect and coexistence. When we listen with empathy, we honor the complexity of human experiences, paving the way for a more inclusive and understanding society. As we work on these skills, we'll find ourselves better prepared to engage in the challenging conversations that shape our lives and communities. Together, let's dedicate ourselves to fostering conversations that not only bridge divides but also shine a light on the shared humanity within all of us.

Influencing Your Circle

Change often starts quietly, like a soft heartbeat beneath the hustle of our daily lives. We might think that the biggest changes in society come from grand gestures or charismatic leaders, but the reality is that true transformation often begins in our closest spaces: our families, friends, workplaces, and communities. Each of us has the incredible ability to be a catalyst for change, influencing those around us in ways that may seem small but can lead to significant impacts over time.

Let's think about how powerful a simple conversation can be. It can act like a gentle push, sparking curiosity in the minds of those we talk to. When we bring up important topics, share interesting resources, or model inclusive behaviors, we start to create waves that can spread far beyond our immediate circle. Change doesn't always need to be loud; sometimes, it's the quiet exchanges that shift perspectives the most.

Leading by example is one of the most effective tools we have. Think about someone who inspires you—not because they have a title or command a crowd, but because they genuinely live their values. It could be a teacher who makes every student feel valued or a neighbor who loves the environment so much that they organize clean-up efforts. Their actions didn't just affect those around them; they encouraged others to reflect on their own behaviors, creating a sense of community and shared responsibility.

Take the story of Sarah, for example. She lived in a neighborhood where community service was pretty much unheard of. One day, she felt inspired to organize a small neighborhood clean-up. She made flyers, knocked on doors, and gathered a few friends to help out. On the day of the clean-up, she was thrilled to see neighbors of all ages show up, some even bringing their kids along, curious about what was happening. As they worked together, conversations naturally unfolded. People shared stories and laughter while picking up litter and beautifying their neighborhood.

That one clean-up didn't just make the area look nicer; it created a sense of community spirit. After that day, discussions about starting a neighborhood garden popped up, and before long, residents began planning a series of seasonal events. The ripple effect of Sarah's simple act grew into something much larger, transforming the dynamics of their community.

What makes Sarah's story so compelling is that it shows how change can start with a single person's choice to step forward. It reminds us that we don't need a platform to make a difference; it often begins with simply showing up and sharing our vision. Each of us has stories and experiences that can resonate with others. By living out the change we want to see, we can invite others to join us on this journey.

If you're thinking about how to inspire change in your circle, consider taking steps that align with your passions and values. Organizing discussion groups around relevant topics is a fantastic way to start. These gatherings can become safe spaces where everyone feels encouraged to share their thoughts. The key is to create an environment where open dialogue is welcomed, and different viewpoints are appreciated.

Imagine starting a book club focused on social justice themes. Each month, you could pick a book that challenges the way we think, exploring subjects like inequality or overlooked historical narratives. As everyone reads and reflects, they'll be prompted to think about their own beliefs. This not only deepens understanding but also sparks meaningful conversations that can lead to concrete actions in their communities.

Also, think about sharing articles, podcasts, or documentaries that highlight pressing social issues. In our digital world, sharing information is easy, and a simple email or social media post can introduce your circle to new ideas. If you find something that resonates with you, don't hesitate to share it. Discussing these shared resources can create an opening for growth and encourage others to reflect on their perspectives.

Community service projects can also be a fantastic way to influence others. By organizing or joining efforts that focus on social justice, you set an example that can inspire others to take action, too. Whether it's volunteering at a local shelter, starting a food drive, or advocating for the environment, these activities can help you connect deeply with your community. When people see you actively participating, they may feel inspired to join in or initiate their own efforts, turning individual actions into collective movements.

The impact of local efforts is immense. History is filled with examples of grassroots movements sparked by passionate individuals. For instance, the civil rights movement in the United States was fueled by many unsung heroes who brought their communities together, organized sit-ins, and led protests. These local actions led to significant societal changes, showing just how powerful individuals can be in driving change.

Social media also offers a unique space for advocacy and connection. While it has its downsides—like echo chambers and misinformation—it also provides amazing opportunities for dialogue and community-building. By using social media thoughtfully, you can amplify your voice and reach more people. Share your insights, engage with others about important issues, and create a supportive online environment where diverse voices are heard.

Imagine starting a Facebook group to discuss local issues. By facilitating respectful conversations, sharing resources, and highlighting community events, you can build a lively online space that encourages collaboration and understanding. Invite group members to share their experiences and ideas, creating a sense of belonging that goes beyond just geographical locations.

As you reflect on your unique abilities and position within your social circles, take a moment to think about how you can actively take part in the ongoing discussions about societal norms and behaviors. Each of us has a role to play, even if we don't always realize it. By engaging, educating, and inspiring those around us, we help move toward a more equitable future.

The Overton Window—a concept that describes the range of ideas the public finds acceptable at any moment—provides a useful lens for understanding how change happens. By influencing our immediate circles, we can gradually shift this window, broadening the boundaries of what's considered acceptable conversation. This shift may be subtle, but it can lead to significant changes in societal norms.

Think about past conversations about issues like marriage equality or climate change. What was once seen as radical has become part of mainstream discourse, largely thanks to the relentless efforts of individuals who dared to challenge the status quo. By engaging in discussions and advocating for inclusivity, we can play a similar role, pushing the boundaries of acceptable thought in our environments.

Remember, change often takes time. While some may wish for quick results, meaningful transformation rarely happens overnight. By creating an atmosphere of open dialogue and genuine curiosity, we lay the groundwork for the seeds of change to take root and flourish.

As we think about our ability to influence those around us, let's acknowledge the power of our words and actions. Every conversation we have, every resource we share, and every project we undertake is part of a larger narrative of progress. Change isn't always a straight path; it can have its ups and downs, but with every step we take, we get closer to a more engaged and fair society.

Ultimately, the challenge is to embrace our roles as change-makers. It's easy to feel overwhelmed by big social issues, but remember that even small actions can lead to significant results. By building relationships, encouraging dialogue, and promoting inclusivity, we can make a lasting impact that goes well beyond our immediate circles.

As you carry this message forward, think about your unique strengths and the ways you can motivate those around you. It all starts with realizing the potential that exists in your relationships. By connecting with others genuinely and sharing your insights, you can spark change that ripples through your community and beyond.

In a world that often feels divided, your voice truly matters. Your actions count. Every time you choose to engage, educate, and advocate for social change, you're playing a part in a collective movement toward a brighter, more inclusive future. So, step into your role as an influencer, and watch as the ripples of your efforts create waves of transformation around you.

Winston Vane

Chapter 10: Shaping the Future—Your Role in Moving the Window

Civic Engagement and Participation

In a world filled with loud opinions, it's easy for one person's voice to get lost in the noise. That's why getting involved in civic engagement and participation is so important. When we connect with our communities, we're not just fulfilling a responsibility; we're gaining a powerful way to make a difference in society. Each of us has a role to play at the crossroads of history, culture, and politics. By actively participating, we can help change the way people think about various issues—what's acceptable or unacceptable in our society.

Civic engagement is the heartbeat of democracy. It's how we share our thoughts, fight for our rights, and join forces with others for common causes. Whether it's going to town hall meetings, casting a vote, or raising concerns on social media, every action helps create a larger story about who we are and what we value. When someone speaks up, they're joining a bigger conversation that can reshape societal norms and behaviors.

Looking back, we can see how grassroots movements have effectively changed minds and policies. Take the civil rights movement in the United States, for example. People from all walks of life came together to demand justice and equality. They organized, marched, and raised their voices against injustice, gradually changing public opinion and influencing laws. This shows us that civic engagement can disrupt the norm and pave the way for real change.

Local government plays a vital part in this process. When citizens engage with their local leaders, they gain a better understanding of their community's challenges. Joining community meetings, taking part in budget discussions, and advocating for local projects are all effective ways to make a real difference. These gatherings give individuals a chance to speak directly to decision-makers and influence the policies that impact their daily lives.

Furthermore, local governments often serve as testing grounds for innovative ideas that might later gain wider acceptance. When new policies like sustainable urban development or progressive social programs are introduced at the city level, they can become blueprints for other places. This shows how local civic engagement can create ripples that help shift public opinion toward ideas that were once considered radical.

In our digital age, technology has transformed how we engage in civic life. Social media, for instance, has made it easier for everyone to share their thoughts and rally support. Platforms like Twitter, Facebook, and Instagram allow individuals to amplify their messages, gather support for causes, and raise awareness about important issues. The quick spread of information online can bring attention to topics that might otherwise be overlooked.

Yet, with this power comes a responsibility. It's important for people to think critically about the information they share, making sure it's accurate and reliable. Misinformation can spread just as quickly, undermining genuine efforts to engage in meaningful discussions. By staying informed and discerning, citizens can use social media effectively to foster discussions that contribute to a broader understanding of various issues.

An equally important aspect of civic engagement is inclusivity. A democracy that truly represents everyone needs voices from all parts of society, especially those who have historically been left out. Engaging with diverse communities enriches the conversation and sheds light on the unique challenges faced by different groups. This builds empathy and understanding, which are crucial for forming coalitions that can advocate for meaningful change.

Getting involved also means volunteering and serving in our communities. By dedicating time and resources to local organizations, people can directly impact the well-being of their neighborhoods. This effort not only strengthens social bonds but also reinforces the idea that change is possible at the grassroots level. When individuals unite for a shared cause—like environmental conservation, education reform, or public health initiatives—they create a sense of purpose that can lead to significant changes.

The personal connections made through civic engagement can result in lasting relationships that go beyond a single project. The friendships and networks formed can sustain movements and provide support during tough times. By building a community of engaged citizens, we create an environment where ideas can thrive, and individuals feel empowered to stand up against injustice.

Participating in civic life is also a learning experience. As people engage in discussions about social issues, they can learn from one another and broaden their perspectives. This exchange of ideas nurtures critical thinking and helps everyone become more informed citizens. When we interact with different viewpoints, we challenge our own beliefs and come to understand complex societal issues more deeply.

Looking at civic engagement and participation, it's clear that everyone has the potential to spark change. The idea of the Overton Window might seem abstract, but it's closely linked to the actions and voices of ordinary citizens. When individuals recognize that their contributions matter, they can harness their collective power to drive real transformations in society.

It's also crucial to acknowledge the history of civic engagement. Various communities have faced unique challenges that have shaped their paths to participation. For instance, people of color, women, and LGBTQ+ individuals have long fought for their voices to be heard in civic life. Understanding these histories equips individuals with the knowledge to advocate for fairness and justice, ensuring that the Overton Window reflects a wider range of perspectives.

As we move further into the 21st century, the global problems we face—like climate change and economic inequality—highlight the urgent need for civic engagement. These complex challenges call for collective solutions and cooperation from all corners of society. When people engage in discussions at local, national, and global levels, they help shape a shared vision for the future that can influence public opinion and policy in ways that once seemed impossible.

In the end, civic engagement is about taking back control. It's about asserting the right to participate in the life of our communities and advocating for the changes we want to see. Every voice counts, and together, we can create a powerful call for justice, equality, and inclusivity. By stepping up to this responsibility, individuals become active creators of their futures, pushing the limits of what's possible and moving the Overton Window toward a fairer and more just world.

As we embark on this journey, it's vital to remember that change takes time. The process of shifting the Overton Window is gradual, often requiring ongoing effort and resilience. History has shown us that persistent advocacy can lead to significant transformations over the years. Movements like civil rights, feminism, and LGBTQ+ rights are all proof of the power of civic engagement. Each of these movements gained momentum through the dedicated work of individuals who refused to accept the status quo.

As we think about our role in shaping the future, let's take on the responsibility of civic engagement with passion and determination. Let's use our voices, actions, and connections to build a society that mirrors the values we cherish. Whether it's organizing in our communities, participating in local politics, or simply discussing important issues with friends and family, every effort matters. The future isn't set in stone; it's a canvas waiting for us to paint our vision of justice, equality, and inclusivity.

Advocacy and Allyship

In the changing world of social justice, advocacy and allyship are like two strong pillars that lift up the voices of those who often go unheard. Advocacy isn't just a popular term; it's the heart of movements that aim to create change. It calls on us to use our voices, our platforms, and our privileges to help those who are often left in the shadows of public conversation. To truly grasp the powerful impact of advocacy, we need to first explore allyship—a promise to stand beside those fighting for their rights, dignity, and place in society.

Being an ally isn't a title you can give yourself; it's something you do through humility, reflection, and actively engaging with the struggles of others. It starts with a basic understanding that privilege shows up in many ways—like race, gender, income, and so on. Recognizing your own privilege is the first step toward being a good ally. This means being ready to listen, learn, and lift up the voices that have been silenced for too long. Real allies don't try to grab the spotlight; instead, they work hard to light the way for others.

Consider the important movement for LGBTQ+ rights. When activists began fighting for marriage equality, they faced a lot of pushback, doubt, and the heavy weight of societal norms that favored heterosexual relationships. It was the allies—friends, family, and advocates from various backgrounds—who stood with the LGBTQ+ community, using their voices and influence to push for change. Celebrities, politicians, and everyday people spoke out to show their support, helping to shift public opinion and ultimately leading to significant legal changes. This shows just how much allyship can matter, not just in terms of visibility but in real-world results.

Being an effective ally also means understanding that the quest for justice isn't one-size-fits-all. What works for one group may not resonate with another. It's crucial to recognize the different contexts and histories that shape the experiences of marginalized communities. For example, fighting against racial injustice is different from promoting gender equality. While there may be some overlap in the broader goals of advocacy, each issue needs its own specific approach. Allies need to be willing to learn about the unique challenges different groups face, ensuring their support is not just well-meaning but also informed and effective.

This understanding leads us to a vital part of allyship: storytelling. Stories have a unique power to connect people, inspire change, and spark conversations. When we share our personal experiences, we create bridges that allow others to walk alongside us, fostering empathy and understanding. Advocacy campaigns that embrace storytelling have proven to be incredibly effective in shining a light on urgent social issues. Take the "It Gets Better" campaign, for instance, which aimed to bring hope to LGBTQ+ youth experiencing bullying and discrimination. By sharing heartfelt stories of resilience, the campaign not only gave a platform to marginalized voices but also encouraged people from all walks of life to stand with the LGBTQ+ community.

Storytelling makes the issues we often discuss feel personal and real. It paints a vivid picture of the struggles individuals face, making it harder for society to ignore them. Through storytelling, we can break down the walls that usually separate us, allowing us to see the humanity in one another. This connection is crucial in advocacy; it turns cold statistics and headlines into real lives, inspiring action that might otherwise remain untouched.

However, using storytelling effectively requires care. Allies must navigate this space responsibly, making sure they don't take over the stories of marginalized communities. True allyship is about lifting others up, not overshadowing them. It's essential to amplify the voices of those directly affected by the issues we're discussing, letting them share their own stories while ensuring they get the recognition and space they deserve. Allies can achieve this by actively listening and creating environments where marginalized individuals feel safe and empowered to share their experiences.

Creating inclusive spaces is another key part of effective advocacy and allyship. Inclusivity goes beyond just having representation; it requires a genuine commitment to welcoming diverse perspectives and experiences. Advocacy efforts should actively seek input from those who are affected by the issues at hand. By nurturing an environment where everyone feels comfortable sharing their thoughts, organizations and movements can better grasp the complexities of the challenges they aim to address.

Yet, the path to inclusivity can be tricky, as many organizations find themselves dealing with challenges like tokenism and performative allyship. Tokenism happens when individuals or groups are included just to meet a diversity goal, without any real investment in their voices or experiences. Performative allyship involves superficial actions—like a social media post or a trendy hashtag—without any real follow-up or support. Both of these practices can undermine the goals of advocacy, as they often lead to disappointment among marginalized communities who see their struggles treated as mere commodities rather than genuinely acknowledged.

To avoid these pitfalls, advocates need to stay alert and self-reflective. This means actively seeking feedback from those they aim to support, recognizing when their efforts fall short, and being open to adjusting their strategies. It also involves a commitment to ongoing learning and growth. The social justice landscape is always changing, and advocates must stay informed about the latest developments and conversations within the communities they aim to uplift.

In the end, advocacy and allyship are ongoing processes that require constant engagement, learning, and flexibility. They aren't just items on a to-do list; they are lifelong commitments to justice and equality. People who choose to stand beside marginalized communities need to recognize that their work doesn't end with a single victory. The struggle for justice continues, and allies have a responsibility to stay active participants throughout this journey, supporting their communities through both victories and challenges.

When we think about the role of advocacy and allyship in shifting the Overton Window—the limits of what society accepts in public discussion—it's clear that every voice can spark change. By using their platforms and privileges, advocates can help reshape societal norms, making space for ideas that were once seen as radical or beyond consideration.

This shift in the Overton Window is a powerful force, as it opens doors to new conversations and possibilities that can lead to real change. When many individuals engage in acts of advocacy, they can inspire larger movements that challenge the very foundations of injustice. This transformative power lies in the hands of those willing to get involved, lift others, and advocate for change.

As we work toward a society that reflects our shared values of justice, equality, and inclusivity, each of us has a part to play. Advocacy and allyship aren't just for activists;

they are responsibilities anyone can take on if they're willing to speak up for the cause. By recognizing the importance of these practices, we can create a ripple effect that encourages others to join the movement.

Let's keep in mind that the journey toward justice is often tough, filled with obstacles and resistance. But just like the civil rights movement arose from a chorus of united voices, our collective efforts can also pave the way for a fairer and more equal world. Advocacy and allyship are not just choices; they are calls to action that urge us to stand together, listen actively, and deeply engage with the issues that matter.

As we navigate this complex journey, let's stay true to the principles of empathy, respect, and understanding. Let's work to create an environment where diverse perspectives are celebrated, where stories are shared and valued, and where the voices of the marginalized are uplifted. By doing this, we not only honor the struggles of those who came before us but also lay the groundwork for a future where justice is more than just a dream; it becomes our reality.

Together, as advocates and allies, we can challenge the status quo, break down the barriers that divide us, and build a society that embraces and celebrates our rich diversity. The road ahead may be tough, but the potential for real change is within reach. By harnessing the power of advocacy and allyship, we can shift the Overton Window and carve out a path toward a brighter, more inclusive future for all.

Envisioning and Building Better Futures

Imagine a world where kindness and compassion are at the heart of everything we do. A place where nobody is left behind, everyone has a voice, and creativity grows hand in hand with fairness. For many of us, this idea might seem like a far-off dream, something that belongs only in our imaginations. But it's through dreaming that we begin to plant the seeds of possibility. Envisioning a better future isn't just a whimsical thought; it's a powerful spark that lights a fire in our hearts and drives us to take action.

As we kick off this journey of envisioning, let's take a moment to ask ourselves some meaningful questions: What kind of world do we want to live in? What values do we cherish, and how can they guide us toward a fairer society? Take a second to reflect on these questions. Picture a society where education is available to everyone, where healthcare is a basic right, and where we protect our environment. Maybe you see a world where the voices of the marginalized are amplified, where we challenge unfair systems, and where working together is more important than competing against one another.

These reflections can motivate us to connect with what matters most. When we take time to imagine the world we want, we're not just daydreaming; we're creating a roadmap for action. This is where hope takes root, turning our dreams into goals we can work toward. It's important to realize that dreams aren't just abstract ideas; they can grow into real movements that change our society. By sharing our visions with others, we build a sense of purpose together—a call to action that resonates with people from all backgrounds.

Throughout history, many significant changes started with a vision that seemed impossible at first. Take the civil rights movement in the United States, for example. It was powered by the dreams of countless individuals who imagined a nation free from discrimination. Martin Luther King Jr.'s famous "I Have a Dream" speech painted a clear picture of a better future, inspiring millions to stand up and demand change. These movements remind us that while dreams may seem small at first, they can energize entire communities and change societal norms.

Turning dreams into action requires creative solutions to the challenges we face. This is where innovation shines, as individuals and groups come up with fresh ideas to solve old problems. From grassroots projects to new social enterprises, there is no shortage of innovative solutions rising up in response to societal issues. A great example comes from sustainable agriculture. As we face climate change and food insecurity, farmers are adopting regenerative practices that not only enrich the land but also produce healthy food for their communities. These farmers aren't just growing crops; they're nurturing resilience, ensuring food justice, and healing ecosystems.

Innovation isn't limited to farming; it spills over into many areas as communities tackle issues from education to healthcare. In cities where accessing quality education is tough, community learning centers have transformed the landscape. These centers tap into local resources, offering tutoring, mentorship, and skill-building workshops to empower young people. By investing in our youth, these initiatives are changing lives, one child at a time.

Think about a community project that tackles homelessness through cooperative housing solutions. Instead of only relying on government programs, creative thinkers have teamed up to build tiny home villages that offer stable homes for those experiencing homelessness. These communities provide shelter and foster a sense of belonging and dignity, encouraging residents to be involved in the decision-making processes. By working together to solve problems, these initiatives show how innovation can come straight from the heart of the community.

As we look at these examples of innovation, it's clear that collaboration is key to success. No one person or organization has all the answers. The best solutions emerge from diverse voices coming together to pursue common goals. When we combine our talents, experiences, and resources, we create a rich environment ripe for creativity and change. This collaborative spirit can be seen in various movements tackling pressing issues, from climate action to racial equity.

Take the climate justice movement, for example. Activists, scientists, policymakers, and community members unite to address the environmental crisis, sharing knowledge and expertise to create comprehensive action plans. By engaging in conversation and tapping into collective intelligence, these groups can make a bigger impact in their communities and beyond. This demonstrates that when people rally around a shared vision, their influence can be massive.

However, as we stand on this exciting path of envisioning and building better futures, we need to recognize that dreaming big isn't enough. Action is what connects our dreams to reality. Turning our visions into practical steps requires guidance that empowers us to make a difference. It starts with understanding the importance of community engagement—an essential ingredient for lasting change.

Community engagement means actively involving people in the decisions that shape their lives. It involves building relationships, listening to different voices, and believing that everyone has a part to play. By creating an inclusive space where all community members feel valued and heard, we can tap into the collective wisdom in our neighborhoods. This approach shifts "us versus them" into "we," fostering a sense of ownership and responsibility that drives us toward shared goals.

Building better futures also means understanding that change takes time. It requires patience, determination, and a willingness to adapt. As we take steps forward, we may face challenges and setbacks. But instead of letting these obstacles stop us, we should see them as opportunities to learn. By adopting a growth mindset—one that sees failure as a stepping stone, not a stumbling block—we can navigate the complexities of social change with resilience and courage.

With the right tools and resources, we can start to create meaningful impacts. Whether it's joining local advocacy groups, attending community workshops, or talking with neighbors, there are countless ways to get involved. Social media can help amplify our voices, share resources, and gather support for the causes we care about. The digital world offers a unique chance for grassroots movements to flourish, breaking down barriers and connecting people who share a vision for change.

We also shouldn't overlook the power of storytelling as a way to inspire action. Sharing our personal journeys, challenges, and successes can resonate with others, encouraging them to join our cause. Stories humanize issues, vividly illustrating the realities we face. They invite empathy and engagement, creating a sense of unity in our shared pursuit of fairness and equity.

As we take action, it's vital to stay connected to our vision, letting it guide our efforts. Visualizing the world we want to create can be a strong motivator, reminding us why we chose to get involved in the first place. Whether it's the dream of a fairer education system, sustainable environmental practices, or inclusive governance, these visions should lead our actions.

In the grand picture of social change, each person adds a unique thread. The beauty of this collective effort lies in its diversity—of ideas, cultures, and experiences that come together to create a more vibrant and inclusive society. As we unite, let's not just dream big; let's also take bold and purposeful steps toward making those dreams a reality. The future we envision is not just a possibility; it's a responsibility we all share.

On this journey toward better futures, remember that we hold the power to shift societal norms and perceptions toward inclusivity and justice. The movements driven by our shared dreams and actions can create ripples that inspire others to join in. Every small act of advocacy and each moment of support contributes to a larger story—a narrative that reaffirms our commitment to a brighter tomorrow.

Ultimately, envisioning and building better futures asks for courage, creativity, and teamwork. It invites us to step outside our comfort zones and actively shape the world around us. While the path may be long and full of uncertainties, the potential for change is within our reach. By dreaming big, embracing innovative solutions, and taking decisive action, we can create a future that reflects our shared values of fairness, equity, and inclusion.

Together, let's rise to this challenge, using our collective strength to question the status quo, nurture hope, and create a world where everyone has the chance to thrive. The journey begins with a vision, fueled by our unwavering commitment to turn that vision into reality. We owe it to ourselves, each other, and future generations to dream boldly and act courageously as we work toward a better world.